"The advice in the sections on fundraising strategies and options is worth the price of the book many times over. It's real-world advice that is based on fact, not theory."

—BRYAN EMERSON,
President and CEO, Starlight Investments,
specialists in early-stage funding

"What makes *Start-Up Smarts* different from any other start-up book out there are the real-world stories from successful entrepreneurs. Not only do these interviews provide guidance and advice; perhaps more importantly, they inspire and show that dreams can come true."

—BOB WATSON,
Senior Vice President, the Ad Council;
former SVP, Newspaper Association of America

"*Start-Up Smarts* is an entertaining read and a solid practical foundation for would-be entrepreneurs. Loaded with timely advice and valuable suggestions, I encourage anyone considering starting a business to read this book to get a head start!"

—MARIA CIRINO,
Co-Founder and Managing Director,
.406 Ventures; Co-Founder, Guardent Security;
former Ernst and Young " Entrepreneur of the Year"

"The Internet and new media are changing the barriers to start-ups everywhere, so the section on the new businesses you can start in today's economy is particularly valuable, timely, and unique. As someone who has seen the impact of major trends in both my dot.com start-up and my recent radio start-up, I know the advice here is particularly important—and just not available anywhere else."

—DAVID GOW,
Founder, Chairman, and CEO,
Gow Communications; former CEO and
CFO of Ashford.com, a publicly traded
online retailer of luxury goods

"This is the book for everyone who thinks they have that "better idea" but doesn't know how to turn it into a business. It is like having a good friend—who has been there before—walk you through every step of the start-up process, calming you down, providing real-world insights, and creating a clear path to success."

—SHIRREL RHOADES,
Editorial Director, *Saturday Evening Post*;
former Executive Vice President,
Marvel Entertainment; former Owner
and CEO, *Opportunity* magazine

START-UP SMARTS

START-UP SMARTS

THE THINKING ENTREPRENEUR'S GUIDE TO STARTING AND GROWING YOUR BUSINESS

BARRY H. COHEN AND MICHAEL RYBARSKI

Avon, Massachusetts

Published by Adams Business, an imprint of Adams Media,
a division of F+W Media, Inc.
57 Littlefield Street, Avon, MA 02322. U.S.A.
www.adamsmedia.com

ISBN 10: 1-4405-0262-5
ISBN 13: 978-1-4405-0262-0

Printed in the United States of America.

10 9 8 7 6 5 4 3 2 1

Library of Congress Cataloging-in-Publication Data
is available from the publisher.

This publication is designed to provide accurate and authoritative information with regard to the subject matter covered. It is sold with the understanding that the publisher is not engaged in rendering legal, accounting, or other
professional advice. If legal advice or other expert assistance is required, the
services of a competent professional person should be sought.
—From a *Declaration of Principles* jointly adopted by a
Committee of theAmerican Bar Association and a
Committee of Publishers and Associations

Many of the designations used by manufacturers and sellers to distinguish
their products are claimed as trademarks. Where those designations appear
in this book and Adams Media was aware of a trademark claim, the designations have been printed with initial capital letters.

This book is available at quantity discounts for bulk purchases.
For information, call 1-800-289-0963.

To our wives, Deborah and Jan . . .

Who, with grace and style, provide us with the support entrepreneurs need—and who are entrepreneurial in their own right. And to our parents, Aaron and Carol Cohen and Walter and Dorothy Rybarski, for doing what it took to provide us with our entrepreneurial DNA.

Acknowledgments

We would like to thank our editors and the staff at Adams Media for their support of this project. We would also like to thank the mentors and business partners we've had who helped shape our entrepreneurial perspective and who have been there when we needed them most. We would also like to thank the many highly qualified experts who have consented to interviews for this book. Their knowledge truly deepens the value you will receive by reading it. The whole is greater than the sum of its parts: Without their combined experiences, abilities, and perspectives, we could not have generated this real-world guide.

"It is not the critic who counts. Not the man who points out how the strong man stumbled or where the doer of deeds could have done better. The credit belongs to the man who is actually in the arena, whose face is marred by dust and sweat and blood; who strives valiantly; who errs and comes short again and again; who knows the great enthusiasms, the great devotions; who spends himself in a worthy cause. Who, at the best, knows in the end the triumph of high achievement, and who at the worst, at least fails while daring greatly, so that his place shall never be with those timid souls who know neither victory nor defeat."

—THEODORE ROOSEVELT
"Man in the Arena" speech
April 23, 1910

Table of Contents

Introduction

EVERY YEAR MORE THAN 600,000 PEOPLE DARE TO START A BUSINESS. Most of those businesses are small—hair salons, restaurants, retail stores; some are mid-sized; and many are done through franchise arrangements. Some aim to create a better life for the entrepreneur and his family; others aim to change the world. About half of them will fail. Yet all of them share this one key characteristic: the entrepreneur is committing himself and taking a risk in a way most people never will. These entrepreneurs are pioneering heroes in many ways, doing things that no one else has done before. Many of them know their task will be difficult. For most of us, business has become a zero-sum game—one in which for someone to win someone else must lose. Competitors, technological innovation, the media, and consumers may all be taking aim at our business goals, armed with new and heavy weaponry. Yet, even in the face of new and more competent competitors, these entrepreneurs say, "I'm in. I want to play." And for many, "I'm betting it all." We applaud and admire you and hope the experiences we and our clients have had can help your chances of success.

We have started businesses ourselves and consulted on start-ups for clients, and found that there are real-world secrets that can accelerate your success, but that too often you only learn these secrets by trial and error. We have seen some of our start-ups succeed beyond any reasonable hope (one of them was the spelling-correction software that most people have used); others ended up about where we hoped, but by different routes than originally planned; and others didn't make it—often because the entrepreneur snatched defeat from the jaws of victory at the last minute.

That's why it's critical to protect your business in as many ways as you can. This doesn't mean there is an absolute way to guarantee success, but there are ways to help you focus on the things that help most and avoid as many landmines as possible. In each chapter, we provide you with at least one real-world secret that will save you thousands of dollars or save you wasted time and focus. As a start, we'll give you a real-world tip right now: Instead of paying a private law firm, you can incorporate your business using electronic forms provided by your state, or through firms like LegalZoom.com, in less than an hour and for much less money. Not only is this faster than working with expensive attorneys, it is generally more accurate because you are using the exact forms provided by the state.

Throughout the book you will find practical tips Smart-Start Tips. You will also see sidebar stories that illustrate each chapter's points. We also bring you expert, real-world advice in a series of interviews with top start-up advisors, and successful entrepreneurs.

You are the person in the arena Theodore Roosevelt admired. You are the person willing to at least explore the option of starting your own business. So to jumpstart your journey, even if you don't read anything else, here's a summary of key tips to entrepreneurial survival that we gained from our own efforts and from the real-world entrepreneurs we've worked with and interviewed.

Keys to Entrepreneurial Survival: An Executive Summary

"I returned, and saw under the sun, that the race is not to the swift, nor the battle to the strong, neither yet bread to the wise, nor yet riches to men of understanding, nor yet favour to men of skill, but time and chance happeneth to them all."

—ECCLESIASTES 9:11, King James Bible Translation

The hard truth is that a significant number of start-ups fail. No matter how skillful we are, no matter how hard we work, no matter how swift or strong or wise, "time and chance happeneth to them all." Start-ups fail for a variety of reasons that include lack of sufficient funding, lack of management experience, and lack of a unique or compelling concept and business idea. They also fail because of bad timing; sometimes a great idea is just a bit too early or a bit too late. Sometimes, even when you do everything right, plain bad luck enters the picture. Time and chance do affect us, so there can never be an absolute way to protect ourselves. Even the most experienced and successful entrepreneurs have often stumbled in their second and third start-ups.

So here's our "Smart-Start" list of some of the most important things to always remember when doing a startup.

Be Flexible with Your Business Plan

If there's one message we heard over and over again from every successful entrepreneur we know, it's that the original plan you create is unlikely to work the way you thought. A rule of thumb that we have created is that every start-up will take longer, need more money, and probably change in some significant way from its original plan. As Mary Frazier, the co-founder of $500 million in assets New Era Life Insurance, said, "The way we succeeded is by searching desperately for something that could generate cash flow when our first three business plans didn't work." That something turned out to be selling Medicare Supplement Insurance, when nobody else seemed interested in doing so. By being open to change, by being flexible, Mary and her business partner, Bill Chen succeeded in ways they could never have planned. Don't worry, keep your eyes open, be flexible, see opportunities when they come, and modify your business to take advantage of those changes. The money counts the same, whether it's from your original plan or a wildly modified one.

Do the Plan—Even Though It Is Likely to Change

Impatient to get on with their great idea or new business concept, many entrepreneurs never slow down enough to create a workable business plan. Just because it is likely to change doesn't mean it's not critical to do a plan in the first place. It is the key to how you will manage and build your business, the essential business management tool. Better to modify a basic plan than not have one at all. In business plans you can create scenarios that will allow you to prepare for changes and contingencies well before they occur. In business you will always have surprises, and even good surprises (too many orders, for example) can be the undoing of an unprepared business. The Boy Scouts are right: It is critical to be prepared, and a good business plan is the key to that.

Pick the Right Industry

According to Professor Scott Shane of Case Western University, author of seven books on entrepreneurship, the industry you choose is critically important to your ability to rapidly grow your business. For example, according to Professor Shane, "The odds that you will make the Inc 500 are 840 times higher if you start a computer company than if you start a hotel or motel." This doesn't mean that if you don't have experience in computers you shouldn't pick that industry; however, you need to shape your expectations for growth and profitability based on the reality of your industry.

Pick the Right Trend

Another way to enhance your chances of success is to ride a trend. For example, two of the businesses we have started focused on a huge demographic trend: the maturing of the so-called baby boomers. Since there are 77 million baby boomers, everything they need as they move through life-stage changes creates new business opportunities. Think about it, Viagra was a joke the first time you saw Senator Bob Dole talking about "erectile dysfunction" in a television commercial. But when 77 million boomers start aging, what was a laughing matter turns into one of the most profitable drugs of all time. Think about all the businesses that will be similarly affected by the aging baby boomers: home health care, nursing, new types of insurance, new clothing, new beds. Demographics are a powerful trend driver, but so are technology, government regulation, and economic conditions. Keep your eyes open: Finding a trend that is rising like a wave is a great way to find start-up success.

Fill the Gaps in Your Management Team or Experience

No matter how experienced, talented, or motivated a manager you are, you can't do it all. We all are stronger at some aspects of business than others. The visionary who can find a new concept before anyone else may not be good at the details of running an accounting system, for example. To increase your chances of succeeding over the long term, surround yourselves with managers and staff who have skills and business perspectives that complement your own. If you want to make sure you don't get off on the wrong path, have people you trust caring passionately about aspects of the business you may ignore or be unable to handle.

Find Guides and Partners

Often there are strategic partners who can help accelerate your growth and take you places you could never get by yourself. There are also experienced professionals who have helped start-up executives and who should be listened to. You may end up disagreeing with their advice, but generally it is good practice to listen carefully to all they say. Remember in all those Western movies, when the arrogant West Point lieutenant ignored John Wayne, it never ended well.

Listen to Your Customer

Perhaps the most important advice we can give is research your concept, test it with potential customers, and listen to what they tell you. Even if you don't like what they say, be open and flexible enough to adapt based on what the customer and the marketplace say. After all, they are always right.

Are Start-Ups Right for You?

Whether you're just starting out in business, or an experienced executive, if you've spent any length of time in one or more careers, or just read about the economic changes we are going through, you know how cyclical business life can be. Few if any of us have had the good fortune to spend our entire working lives in an industry insulated from economic woes. Imagine gaining control of your own destiny; knowing that every day, when you put the key in the door, no one can eliminate your division, your department, or your position. Those are the positives. On the other hand, starting businesses isn't for everyone.

SMART START TIP:

Learn Before You Earn

Many have said you should learn from your mistakes. We say learn from others' mistakes; it's a lot cheaper. Before you venture out on your own, work for others — more than once — in a business like the one you want to own. Each time you look over another set of shoulders, you will learn more about the right and wrong way to run a business.

To be an entrepreneur, you need a superior business idea, enough stamina to meet the high demands of entrepreneurship, and the burning passion to pursue success relentlessly. There will be sacrifices. Often you will be working longer hours, and incurring more stress than any employee. Ultimately, and most importantly, while the rewards are there for you, so are the risks. It's not for the faint of heart. But if you have the heart for it, it can be the most rewarding career choice you ever make.

How Deep Are Your Pockets?

The cost to acquire a going concern can often prove prohibitive. Anyone selling you a business with a track record and solid potential will want a fair price. When you and your advisors (yes, you need a team to do this right) evaluate their business, you may well determine that either the asking price is simply too rich for your blood or the return on your investment simply will not materialize. Today, in our service-sector driven economy, many industries' start-up costs are not overwhelming. As a result, the time it takes to recoup the initial investment and reach profitability is shorter. We call this circumstance "reduced barriers to entry." We will discuss this in greater depth later. For example, if you decide to engage in e-commerce, you have eliminated many of the costs of a brick and mortar business—such as storefronts, possibly warehousing, inventory, personnel, etc. More than ever before, with the right business concept and the right promotion, people can start-up and succeed quickly.

O Say Can You See . . .

Nothing is more American than seeking, achieving, and maintaining independence. As an entrepreneur when you put that key in the door, you answer only to your clients and your investors . . . if you have any. When you work for others, you have no control over your time. Someone dictated how you spent your time—often to justify his or her job. As an entrepreneur you have 100% control of your time—you can decide whether to start working at 5 A.M. or 5 P.M. To many of us, that independence alone is worth all the work and the struggles.

What Are You Building?

As if control of your destiny didn't have a high enough value, try this on for size: You can't build any equity by working for someone else. We all know that you might earn more money on a job than you can take out of your business, until it becomes really profitable. However, we also know that almost all people spends at or above their means. So if you work for someone else at a job, when you approach retirement, at best, you may have a well-funded retirement account—maybe. Conversely, if you follow the formulas for business success, you live within your means during the critical formative years while you are nurturing your business, you create value in your business, and you have a proper exit strategy, you will have built equity in your business instead of building it for someone else. For many entrepreneurs—especially the mid-life variety—that in itself makes it worthwhile.

SMART START TIP

Start-Ups Are Longer, More Expensive, More Difficult, and Different Than You Plan

To achieve your goals, no matter how realistic you think your plan is, it will probably take longer, cost more, be harder, and end up working in a different way than you thought. This is a hard lesson to internalize, but in start-ups things rarely work the way you plan. Of course, you should plan based on your best guess then build a contingency plan based on doubling every aspect of it.

The Entrepreneurial Mindset

Not everyone will do this; not everyone can do this. Armed with determination, a superior business concept, a solid plan, many can execute a business start-up and achieve success. However, the one remaining deciding factor that separates those who will from those who won't is "DNA." Some of us just plain have it in our genes; others don't. It may not be actual genetic mix, but there is something special and unique that distinguishes the people who are willing to take entrepreneurial risk from those who are happy being someone else's employee.

Make no mistake: DNA matters; it figures into the entrepreneurial success equation. So just what is this entrepreneurial mindset or genetic makeup? It means that when the factory whistle blows, you're still at your workstation. It means you work until the work is done when you have a deadline. It means you trundle in to work even when you don't feel your best. It means you set your alarm clock an hour earlier to fight your way through traffic, and love it—because you're going exactly where you want to go, to do exactly what you want to do, every day.

Chapter

1

Bulletproof Your Business Concept

Once you've decided you might want to be an entrepreneur, the first thing you need to do is decide what kind of business you want to be in. You must test your concept to see if it has what it takes to succeed in a timeframe that makes financial sense.

Most people who come to us with new business ideas or plans are infused with a passion and have a strong belief that they are sitting on El Dorado just waiting to be mined. The enthusiasm and passion are there, often expressed in phrases like, "Everyone needs this" or "Nobody's doing this yet" or "This is going to be the next big thing."

The enthusiasm is admirable, but it's at this point it's good to remember how enthusiastic the members of the Donner Party were about getting to California. Unfortunately, as you may remember, the Donner Party was a group of pioneers looking to make their fortune in the new land of California. Everything about their concept looked great. Except for one thing—they didn't count on an earlier than expected winter, got stuck in what is now known as Donner Pass, and ended up starving to death, after first resorting to cannibalism. Their concept was great. Their timing was misjudged. To do a successful start-up, you have to take into account more than just one variable, and having a great concept is just one of them.

SMART START TIP

Test, Test, Test!

Test all contingencies — including the power of your concept and the timing of what it takes to make it happen.

You might say what the Donner Party should have done is gotten a guide who knew when and how to make it safely through the mountains to the Paradise on the other side. Here's the other lesson—they did have an experienced guide who told them it was too late in the season to try to cross the mountains. He told them absolutely they would never make it and starve.

THEY DIDN'T LISTEN TO HIM.

To make sure your venture into start-ups leads to celebratory dinner parties and not Donner parties, it's key to plan and test and look at as many contingencies as possible as early and as often as possible, do all the research you can, and listen to experienced guides who can help you achieve success.

SMART START TIP

Listen to Your Guides

When you hire an experienced guide, listen to him.

Now, you may think, "Wait a minute, I know my idea can work—it's great—let's get on with it. How can I smart start my concept?" We say fabulous, let's begin with the smart-start policy.

Smart-Start Your Concept: Ask Three Questions

According to *BusinessWeek* magazine's rating of graduate schools of business, the number one business school in America is at the private university founded by John D. Rockefeller, the University of Chicago. If you spent the money to go to the University of Chicago and take a class from Harry Davis, the Roger L. and Rachel M. Goetz Distinguished Service Professor of Creative Management, here's what you would learn.

Before you start any business ask these three questions:

1. Who are your customers?

2. What do they really want?
3. How do you know?

Now since it's absolutely key to making your concept succeed, let's look at those questions in some detail.

Who Are Your Customer?

So many of the entrepreneurs we have worked with assume that because they love their idea for a business or product, everyone else will too. Unfortunately, that just isn't the case. For one thing, most people are already using something to satisfy whatever need you think is now unmet. Getting people to change from what they are already using or doing is rarely easy. Even if you have something that is better, it's hard to get people to change from what they already do or use—that's the power of existing products and brands. When Dell came out with easier-to-buy and less-expensive personal computers, they still had to convince people to change from their comfort with brands like IBM and Compaq.

When you think about your target customer, can you picture exactly who that is? Picture and describe your ideal buyers: how old are they? What gender? Where do they live? How much money do they make? Are they working or are they retired? Do they have children? What ethnicity, race, or cultural characteristics do they have?

You may be able to describe your buyers in detail and then conclude that there are other target buyers for your product as well. Describe them in detail as well. Once you have really clear pictures of your customers, write them down in detail. Then ask yourself how many of these people there are and how many of them are in your geographic target area.

The idea of identifying your customers is absolutely critical to shaping every aspect of your business concept; nothing you do will be more important. And just remember, it's so important that even the biggest companies spend a huge amount of time with consultants and data firms trying to define who their customers are and who they will be in the future.

Starbucks' customers come in a variety of types, and they may actually buy different products. Some may come for the coffee, others for the "Starbuck experience," others for a place to socialize. But as successful as Starbucks is, not everyone is a Starbucks customer.

What Do They Really Want?

Now that you've got a detailed image of who your customer is or may be, it's time to get specific about what they want. This may not be as obvious as you think. For example, EmLogis, a company our friend Marty Estill helped co-found, created a scheduling software product that looked like an obvious winner. Their proprietary software has an algorithm that schedules staffing for hospitals, retail stores, and any firm that needs to schedule more than thirty employees.

EmLogis's benefits seemed incontrovertible: It was proven to save companies as much as 30 percent of their salary costs and gave employees scheduling that met their individual needs. Who wouldn't buy this product? Well, it turns out that the buyers of the product were not the users of the product, and that there was a third customer in the mix whose needs had nothing to do with savings or happier employees.

In the EmLogis case, and in the case of business-to-business sales in general, the buyers, users, and person that benefits the most may all be different. The barrier to EmLogis's immediate success was that while the CFO wanted the savings it produced and the employees wanted the flexibility and comfort it gave them with schedules that matched their individual requests, the administrators who actually made the schedules felt threatened by the lack of control this new technology seemed to represent.

Great savings, happier employees, higher profits—and it still wasn't enough to accelerate the sale of EmLogis through many large corporate bureaucracies. After four years of hard work, and the development of hard-measured results and training materials that addressed the fear of change that was the hidden barrier to sales, EmLogis is now getting the sales traction that can make it a great return for its investors.

How Do You Know?

As we've worked through various start-ups and turnaround situations, we always begin by interviewing the founder or management team. When we ask, "Who's your customer?" we frequently get a strong answer. It looks like most founders of companies and managers have thought about who their customer is, and many of them have strong opinions about it.

When we ask, "What does your customer want?" we also get answers, but from fewer managers. The obvious answer—they want our product—doesn't really get you anywhere, and few entrepreneurs have thought about what their customers really want. Many of them will say, "Well, they will want my new product or service; it's obviously better" (or cheaper or more convenient or more powerful).

When we ask, "How do you know?" that's where things get awfully quiet or awfully emotional.

Because the truth is, most managers or entrepreneurs have never taken the time or figured out ways to verify who their customer is or what they want. The answers we often get are, "I've been doing this for a long time, and I just know what they want" or "Everyone will want this product or benefit." It's easy to assume that your individual passion or belief is shared by many, but it's the most dangerous of all business assumptions.

Remember the dot.com boom and then the dot.com bust? It was one of the most incredible wealth transfers in our history. Entrepreneurs were everywhere. Business plans written on napkins were getting million-dollar funding. Much of the boom, and all of the inevitable bust, was based on one simple yet very flawed, belief: that somehow, if you built a business, people would come to it, would find their way to it—even without advertising or other promotion. While this field-of-dreams approach made an emotionally powerful basis for a fun movie, the premise caused billions of dollars to be invested and then lost because there was no evidence that customers would come just because you built it.

Do You Want the Truth?

There are easy, inexpensive, and low-risk ways of testing your assumptions about your customers and what they want, but many entrepreneurs don't want to know the truth. If you think this couldn't be true, remember the dot.com boom. We'll use one we'll call "GrandMA.com" (not the actual company name) as an example, a company created without a clear vision of the customer and what they wanted.

"GrandMa.Com": A $7 Million Investment in a Company with No Customers

GrandMa.com was based on the emotionally compelling idea that grandmothers would like to communicate with their computer-literate grandchildren—emotionally compelling, and true for many grandmothers, no doubt. The problem was the assumption of the company that these grandmothers would choose to do this communicating via the Internet using a personal computer. Since this seemed obvious to the computer-literate grandchildren who were the founders of this company and all their computer-literate friends, it never occurred to them to ask whether any of those grandmothers actually owned computers, could access the Internet, or had even heard of it. Remember, this was in the late nineties when the World Wide Web was a new phenomenon and its use was restricted to highly technical early adopters. Because they believed their grandmothers were like them, they believed they would be attracted to this technology as well. That was just not the case, and $7 million later, with no real sales and no real customers, this company disappeared. Years later, when grandmothers are using computers, this idea can be a winner. Again, timing, and understanding who your customers really are, are key.

SMART-START TIP

Ask and You Shall Receive

Remember, you are not your customer.
To find out what they want, you have to ask them.

Smart-Start Research on a Dime

We've established that market research is one of the most important things you can do for your company. However, you might be sitting there saying, "Wait a minute, I'm an entrepreneur, not a millionaire. I can't afford market research or consumer studies." There's a reason why you might make assumptions about who your customers are and what they want: You probably think there's no affordable way to find out what they really want.

Your reaction is understandable, and frankly, even at very large companies with big marketing and sales budgets, there is an almost cult-like reluctance to do the research into customer behaviors or desires that might undermine long-held beliefs. But the risk of not understanding what your customers really want, and the success you can get by giving them exactly what they want, make it worthwhile to make sure you become an expert on who they are and what they want. Fortunately, there are simple and inexpensive ways to learn about your customers, if you really want to.

Focus Groups

Qualitative research is just a fancy term for talking to your customers in somewhat informal ways. The most common ways to do this research is through interviews or in group interviews with eight to ten potential customers, in what is known as a focus group. It can cost you very little to target prospective customers and review your concept with them. Start with individuals you can recruit through family or friends, and then move to convention or mall settings where you can talk to truly independent potential customers who will spend ten or fifteen minutes with you just because you ask. You can also offer a small honorarium for participating. In one recent convention situation, we were able to obtain 150 interviews from random prospective customers just by asking and saying that their participation would enter them in a drawing for free flowers. People are often very willing to give you their opinions, especially since so few entrepreneurs seem to really want to know and are sincerely interested in answers that may not be what they were expecting.

A few guidelines to structuring your interviews:

1.   Describe your concept in simple sentences that might be the basis for an ad. (If your prospective customers can't understand your concept they certainly won't be able to purchase it.)
2.   Ask what your prospective customers are already using to provide the service or benefit you are proposing.
3.   Describe why your product or service is better.
4.   Track the honest reactions from your interviewees. If they don't understand it or want it don't blame them or ignore them. It may mean you have to refine how you present your concept or change aspects of it.
5.   Listen carefully to the positive and negative comments they make. Your prospective customers can be the key to giving you the language and benefits that will make your product a must buy for them.

6. As you listen, revise your benefit statement and business description. The goal here is to get warm . . . warmer . . . warmest. Let's assume that your original business concept has real merit. Talking to prospective customers can help you understand how you can make it even better for them and how you can communicate your benefit in ways they understand.

7. Listen for barriers to your success. Be sure you listen especially to "but" sentences or "if they did this" or "I would buy it except" statements. This means you're probably on to something that is attractive to your target buyers, but there is something you need to revise or improve.

If after completing a number of research interviews you sense that there are real customers for your product or business, refine that business concept in ways that allow you to trial sell your product.

Trial Selling

This is the reverse of the "If you build it they will come" concept. We say instead, "If they will come, you should build it." And the really good news is that it is far less expensive to find out if customers will buy your product than it is to build a product or open a restaurant or retail store and then find out nobody really wants what you have built.

Now, what you may not know is that major marketers of products you use do this kind of testing all the time. They do what is known as dry tests in direct mail and test marketing in retail.

Here are some ways you can do similar trial selling yourself.

Hire Unlikely Researchers to Work for You

If you're creative, there are always ways to find your prospective customers and test concepts with them. If you don't believe us, here's a true story of how we gained over 400 surveys (quantitatively valid) from very affluent, hard to reach, upwardly mobile young business executives. Such research would normally be very expensive and difficult to obtain; however, we were able to get this statistically valid testing done for sixty dollars and a few Happy Meals. First, create products to trial sell. A few years ago, one of us was looking to launch a magazine. The magazine was conceived to target younger-generation business people—ambitious, excited, and affluent, or about to be. A great deal of qualitative research indicated that the concept seemed strong and prospective customers, young men and women, seemed positive in their response. But qualitative research isn't enough. To trial sell the magazine, we created sample covers with a list of over 200 potential cover articles (the real product in a magazine is the cover and the four or five articles that call out to the potential buyer). On survey sheets, we listed sample covers and all 200 articles (potentially forty months worth of covers). We asked the prospective customers to rate the articles from "I would definitely buy the magazine just to read this one article" to "I'm not interested at all in this article."

You may be asking how you get hundreds of trial sales without spending thousands of dollars. Well, here's one secret: Hire a bunch of sixth graders to do the research for you. No, we're not joking. For the start-up magazine we mentioned above, that's just what we did. My stepson asked six of his girl classmates if they would like to have some fun, make a little money, and get a free lunch helping his step-dad on a project. They loved the idea, and they were the perfect people to get research when nobody else could. So the next day our research project began. We took a van of these young people to Harvard Business School (we were living in Boston at the time), armed those girls with sample covers, test survey articles, and the request they were supposed to make of the professors that were teaching classes. Would it surprise you to learn that every single professor was willing to interrupt their classes and let their students fill out the surveys? In a couple of hours we had over 400 completed test-sales surveys which ranked over 400 articles on the "would definitely buy" scale.

If I had tried to get this information using professional surveyors, we probably couldn't even get any of these busy people and professors to stop and fill out one form. But who could say no to polite, earnest, and charming sixth-grade girls? In addition, there was the surprise factor—those little girls weren't supposed to be there, they weren't typical researchers. That fact alone disarmed the interviewees and made them give more thoughtful answers than they would have normally. Most importantly, for less than $100 we were able to trial sell more than 400 magazine article titles and offers to buy the magazine. By the way, the results were very positive.

Run Direct Mail or Direct Response Ads

Another way to trial sell your concept or product is to build direct mail or space ads that offer your product exactly as if you were in business. This is an accurate way to find out if people will buy your product. It costs very little to create an exact ad or direct mail piece, rent a mail list, and mail out those packages to see what kind of response rate you get. Or you can create ads and run them in the classified section of newspapers or magazines that would reach your customers. One of our good friends, Shirrel Rhoades, one of America's most experienced direct marketers, would always test his concepts with short classified ads in a national magazine. The classified ads cost less than $200, but he would get to test about 100,000 potential customers. Granted, the classified ad was small and only reached a small portion of the readers, but he could find out for sure if there were real buyers for his products. Magazine and other direct-mail marketers do this all the time—they call it doing dry tests. They also may offer different versions of the ads to test a variety of aspects of their products. For example, you may want to offer three or four ads, each exactly the same except for a change in only one of the following factors:

1. Test the Price (Higher or Lower)
2. Test the Offer (Whatever you are using to inspire a response—a discount, free gift, etc.)
3. Test the Headline

There will be more on this kind of testing in Chapter 6, but for now, it is enough to say that you can learn a tremendous amount for very little. Most important, you can find out if using the marketing materials you would actually use to launch your business generates customers.

Let's say the dry tests were a great success and a large number of people order your nonexistent product. What do you do now? Simple, you include their names in your database (as simple as an Excel spreadsheet) as future customers. Then you send them a thank-you letter saying they were part of a test, that you appreciated their interest, that you will contact them when you launch your business, and you may also give them a gift for participating. That gift, by the way, should most often be a discount on their future purchase of your products.

Trial selling is the best way to ensure your concept and is on track with what customers want. It works in a variety of ways, whether your product is a consumer product for the masses or a specialized business-to-business product or service. In any case, you can create prototype ads that are your best effort to sell your product or service and run those ads or mail them as a representative sample to as many of your prospective buyers as possible.

In summary, the key to making your concept succeed is to always ask the three questions, research them with prospective customers, refine your concepts based on input from initial research, and then trial sell your concept and refine your selling model and offer based on multiple tests.

Smart-Start Summary: *Tips to Bulletproof*
Your Concept

1. Avoid the "If we build it they will come" fallacy.
2. Reverse the model and "Test it, and see if they will come, then build it."
3. Listen carefully, and test and refine your concept based on customer input all the time.
4. Remember, ego is your enemy.
5. You are not your customer.
6. Not everyone is your customer.
7. Ask the three questions:
   a. Who are your customers?
   b. What do they want?
   c. How do you know?

Chapter

2

Develop a Smart-Start Business Plan

Now that you've tested your concept and are convinced that you have a business or product people will want, need, and buy, the next step is to map out how you turn that concept into a functioning business.

Just having customers who want your product doesn't mean you can succeed as a business. You now have to address a detailed list of questions and formulate answers and strategies that allow you to fund, staff, and launch your business. The best way to do that is to create a formal business plan that lets you address key issues in advance. There are a couple of things about any business plan that will almost always be true: The plan will change. It will often take more money than you thought. It will almost always take longer than you plan. Sometimes, very rarely, things work better than planned, and when that happens, count your blessings. But whatever you do, plan. We've heard over and over from successful entrepreneurs: " I don't believe in plans; I believe in planning."

The creation of a really good plan is not easy, and you need to be brutally hard with yourself as you address the issues you must resolve in this plan. But there's an upside—when you've created a good plan, you and your team have taken a big step on the way to achieving your success. You will know where you need to go and what you need to do. There will always be sur-prises and adaptations required, but you now have your key management and measurement tool in place.

The Business Plan Outline

There are many variations on the theme of a business plan. Depending on the complexity of your business concept and the size of the business you envision, you may end up with a ten-page plan or a fifty-page plan. No matter the length of your plan, however, virtually every business plan we have ever seen will address in some detail the issues listed below. The order in which you do so also may vary, but here's an outline that has worked for us and many of our clients. Remember, creating your business plan is not just an exercise, it is the critical tool that can show you your path to success. Take your time on this, and treat this exercise as if your start-up success depended on it. It does.

The Executive Summary

The executive summary will be the two most important pages you may ever write. The executive summary is the first impression you will make on your prospective investors, potential management members, and strategic partners. It is the ad for your new business. If you cannot sell the concept in these two pages, you never will. If you are trying to raise money, gain bank financing, or get credit or terms for your new business, everyone you deal with will ask you for your executive summary. The rest of the business plan will show you've done your homework.

A rule of thumb is that the executive summary should never be more than two pages long. For that reason, you need to write it only after every other section of the business plan has been completed. It has to be the distillation of all the thought and work done in the rest of the plan. As an entrepreneur, and almost by definition, someone who wants to break new ground, you may be asking why only two pages.

The simple answer is that's what everybody who will fund your business or partner with your business or support your business will ask for—not a complete business plan, but first, your executive summary. And if you can't sell them on the power and the opportunity for success in two pages, you won't be able to sell them in forty.

One of our friends, Bryan Emerson, is the Chairman of Starlight Capital, a group that organizes venture seminars at the Yale Club to link entrepreneurs and venture groups. Bryan has linked more than fifty entrepreneurs with funding sources, and places such a strong emphasis on the power of the executive summary that he requires a specific format and style. It features a summary of the key sections of the business plan as well as lists of your banks, accountants, and legal advisors. As complete as the information it provides is, it's never more than two pages.

Market Opportunity and Size

This section of the plan is based on the concept research and testing you've already done. **The most compelling point you can make in convincing others to support your vision is to show them that your concept is one that consumers are ready to buy.** The evidence you have as qualitative research and trial-selling evidence will be tremendously useful in gaining interest, support, and financing. The other aspects of the opportunity you will want to emphasize here are not only the passion your consumers have for your product, but also the size of the audience. If the market is growing or can be expected to grow, that is important as well. Riding a trend is a great way to ensure your start-up is fail-proof.

We call it finding a Bozo Business—a business that even Bozo the clown could succeed in because the supporting trend is so strong. When Steve Jobs started Apple, he and his partner Steve Wozniak weren't strong managers, but they were in front of a trend for an easy-to-use home computer that was so powerful that their growth was legendary. They could have failed in many ways. There were many times they didn't have enough inventory and their financial management wasn't impeccable, but they were in front of a powerful trend for smaller, easy-to-use computers, and demand for their product trumped every other aspect of business management.

Trying to launch even a great product in a market that is static or declining is a much tougher play. If your business is in a market in which, for you to win, all of your competitors have to lose, that is a particularly difficult environment in which to launch a business. You're in a zero-sum game, and that is a very difficult proposition. If at all possible, find business opportunities where the market is growing so that you can win, even when other competitors win as well. A rising-tide market is easier for you, your investors, and your partners to accept and succeed in.

Find Markets That Are Growing

Having a strong customer demand that you can demonstrate from your research and a large or growing market make a powerful combination when you are trying to raise money to fund your business.

Product Definition and Strategy

This is where you describe your product in detail, and why consumers are going to want it. Here you'll explain what your core product and your augmented product are, which will include price, emotional context, and the ultimate reward a consumer gains by purchasing it. A good example of the core product at Starbuck's might be fine and differentiated coffees. The augmented product at Starbuck's is a much more complex proposition, and might include the environment, the music, comfortable chairs, T-mobile wireless computer access, and groundbreaking high prices.

Competition

Michael was chairing a venture seminar hosted by a number of leading business-school alumni clubs. There were a number of venture experts on the panel, and they made interesting and complementary points on what funders looked for in a business plan they would fund. Without exception, however, every panelist mentioned that the number one reason for rejecting a business plan for funding was a lack of attention to the competition. As one panelist noted, "We have an iron-clad rule: If you don't know your competitors inside out, we will not fund that business." This makes obvious sense, except to many entrepreneurs.

A classic line we have heard hundreds of times from these passionate pioneers is, "There is no competition. We're the first at what we do" or, "We're so much better, cheaper, (insert any one of a thousand adjectives) that nobody can compete with us." Often, these entrepreneurs will not even have a section on competition in their business plans. We can assure you that every business has competitors, and figuring out how you are going to overcome them is absolutely critical to having a successful start-up.

Ways to develop your competitive set and create strategies to overcome your competition will be described in depth in Chapter 6, but understand this—one simple way to make your business plan stand out from most, and thereby enhance your chance of being funded, is to have an outstanding section in your business plan on the competition.

Marketing Strategy

This is the section of your plan where the research and testing you did on your product concept will pay off. You will also reference your competitive set and outline your strategies for addressing the 4 Ps of marketing: Product, Price, Place, and Promotion. You will also demonstrate what so many of the dot.com entrepreneurs never knew—marketing is different from sales, and you need to have clear and powerful strategies for both.

Sales Strategy

It was hardly more than a decade ago when business logic ceased to apply for a significant period of time. In this case, we're referring to the fact that we worked with a number of entrepreneurs who ultimately received significant venture funding, and who, when they first approached us, didn't even have a sales section in their business plan. They had beautifully articulated ideas about how great their new product was going to be and how it had no competition. They also explained how everyone would want it. When you asked them exactly how the product was to be sold, they gave a blank stare and the "Everyone will buy it" response. In this section of your plan, you will be talking about sales channels, partnership and relationship strategies, referral models, repeat sales, and overall customer-relationship management.

SMART-START TIP

Manage Entrepreneurial Stress

There's no doubt that starting a business can be extremely stressful. There's no way to avoid the pressure of a start-up; however, you must remember to stay healthy. Diet, sleep, and exercise all play an important part in your small business success. If you aren't healthy, your business won't be healthy.

Production and Delivery Strategy

Here you will demonstrate how you plan to produce (or acquire) the products you plan to sell, and what it will cost you to do so. You'll also be talking about how you will inventory those products and ship and deliver them to your customer. You will have to address the issues of scalability and preparation for rapid growth, and the margins you can achieve every time you sell. The good news here is that in the last seven years alone, there has been incredible progress in the development of virtual partners who can help with almost every aspect of product development, warehousing, management, and shipping and delivery. Remember, some of the best-known companies in America, like Amazon and Dell, created huge businesses without owning a warehouse, inventory, or a truck to deliver their products.

Management, Infrastructure, and Support Systems

Every venture funder you will ever meet will tell you that what they look for in a business plan is the strength and size of the opportunity, the strength and validation of the concept, and the strength of the management team. And of these three, the conventional wisdom is that management is most important of all. What we've seen, however, is that what really gets funders' attention is the strength and size of the opportunity and the product concept and its validation. If the concept is attractive enough, venture funders will actually work with you to develop or expand a management team. And there are so many ways to outsource management and staff that you can be significantly virtual in the development of your support functions like human resources, accounting, taxes, and insurance. What you need to do in this section of the plan, however, is still extremely important. You have to show that you have the management team, experience, and ability to execute the plan in every function. Outsourcing management and staff may actually help in your launch by making costs variable and predictable. We believe that when funders stress the quality of management, what they're really looking for is the entrepreneur's passion and commitment to succeed in this business. Here is the place where your enthusiasm and passion should be unleashed.

Risks

The sections of business plans that most entrepreneurs don't want to write, or even acknowledge, are the sections on competition and risks. Yet, if approached correctly, these are the sections that can allow you to really reflect on key issues that could prevent your success. One way to think about this section is to list your barriers to success. By creating such a list you can also create ways to overcome these barriers. Every business has risks or barriers that can get in the way. Creating a list of what those barriers might be and ways to overcome them should be an exercise that has a calming effect. The fact that you have addressed barriers to success will certainly boost your investors' confidence in you.

Exit Strategy

This doesn't have to be a long section or even a formal part of the plan. However, you, your management team, your business partners, and certainly your investors will want to get a sense of why you are doing this business and what you expect to receive from it. If you are raising money from investors, the single most important issue for them is what they get out of it. You may want to run and operate a business, but your investors are going to want to know the financial return they will receive. You also may have several answers that show directionally where you want to go. For example, saying that you want to build something and sell it leads to options like private company acquisition or an IPO (initial public offering.)

Financial Plan

Here's where you create detailed profit and loss statements, cash flow forecasts, and balance sheets. Sure, they're *pro formas*, which means they're just projections, but they should be as accurate as you can make them. You will be using these forecasts as you raise money to answer questions with your banks, value your business, and evaluate your performance compared to plan. As they work on these projections, many people find it easier to take multiple approaches—conservative, aggressive, and best-guess models. While it's impossible to predict the future, it's important to work as hard as possible to make these forecasts as accurate as they can be.

Exhibits

This last section is where you get to add some sizzle to your plan. Here's where you may want to insert evidence pieces that might include summaries and samples from your market research, ad pieces, marketing materials, supply chain charts, and any other materials that bring your plan to life and show that you are ready to launch your business.

Smart-Start Summary: Keys to Creating a Smart-Start Business Plan

1. Describe your business concept, plan of execution, its advantages for your customers and the returns investors will receive, in a two-page executive summary. Write it last; present it first.
2. Tackle the tough points—your competitive landscape and the risks.
3. Tell your prospective investors when they can expect a payback and how much.
4. Even if you know your plan will change, believe in planning.
5. Your business plan is not just a tool to raise money. It is the key tool to managing your business.

3

New Ways
to Attract
Your Funding

There are numerous options for financing your start-up and later growth. Which one or ones are right for you? Let's explore the benefits and risks of each so you and your team of advisors can make the right choices. Here are just a few of the considerations we will examine:

- How much do you give up?
- What are the dangers of dilution?
- How do you value your business?
- How do you reward your investors?
- What are the exit strategies for both you and your investors?
- Who defines your business's success and how?

Interestingly, the answers to many of these questions come from the very first question you might ask yourself: Why am I doing a start-up? If you are doing a small restaurant, franchise, or service business, the answer might be that you just want a career where you are the boss and have a chance to make a reasonable living. For many entrepreneurs that is the key motivation. Owning a business that they can manage for many years and perhaps pass on to their heirs is a big part of the American dream for many folks.

On the other hand, for younger entrepreneurs who have grown up on Silicon Valley success stories and who have heard about billion-dollar market caps for start-ups like MySpace or Facebook, the answer may be all about the exit strategy: How do I start a company that other people will buy from me for a lot of money? All of the answers to the financing questions will ultimately be shaped by what your philosophy about your firm is. Are you an owner and operator or a builder and seller? And what is the timeframe for your exit strategy? If you want to own for a long time, all the financing issues will be answered differently versus an entrepreneur who would like to build and sell over a three- to five-year horizon. Of course, there is a middle ground, where you may build and sell part and still be a significant owner and key operator. Now let's look at the financing issues that may be appropriate for each type of entrepreneur:

Your Personal Money: The Bootstrappers (Often Owner/Operators)

Some of us have been fortunate enough to start businesses that don't require a huge capital investment for start up. Typically, these are in the service sector. If your space, equipment, and staff requirements are small, you may be able to fund it out of pocket. The upside for the bootstrappers is obvious: You don't answer to legions of investors. The downside: You often pit ourselves against larger, more established, and better-funded competitors during the start-up phase. However, bootstrappers are often nimbler than their counterparts and can weather the downturns better with lower overhead.

At some point, even if you started the business with your own money and even if it appears to be somewhat self-funding from the revenue generated, you will probably need to tap into additional financing to grow the business. Your obvious advantage: You will probably turn a profit sooner—or at least pay yourself sooner. Just make sure you have calculated all of your expenses properly. It becomes even more critical to have an accurate picture of your expected operating costs when your start-up funds are not only limited, but finite.

Salim Omar, MBA, CPA, and author of *Straight Talk About Small Business Success*, advises entrepreneurs to, "Use their own money first; go to their circle of acquaintances next." He poses the question: "Whom do you want to be accountable to?" suggesting that having lenders and investors will induce you to produce results, yet also create pressure. He stresses the importance of communicating properly with them so they don't end up interfering with the operation.

Other People's Money: How Does it Work?

Once you have determined how much you need for your start-up, exactly how that money will be used, how much of your own resources you are prepared to invest, and how and when you can repay your investors, you need to determine which sources are the best prospects for your type and size of business. This involves assessing each potential sources' degree of risk tolerance. Let's take a look at your potential pool of investors:

+ Banks
+ Private investors
+ Public offerings
+ Government agencies

Jeff Bunin, a loan officer with Capital Lending Inc. of North Bergen, New Jersey, also serves as an adjunct instructor at Rutgers University. Jeff categorically states: "The SBA (United States Small Business Administration) should be the lender of last resort—not your first choice."

Although many SBA loans are offered through local banks and are underwritten (funded) by the federal government, they have stringent requirements—most notably, good collateral. Several years ago, a local Chamber of Commerce official called us in a frantic effort to help a member whose business had taken a downturn. Outfitted with fancy offices, the owner had financed his business with an SBA loan secured by his home. He was desperate to sell off furniture, phone systems, and anything else to raise quick cash to save his home from foreclosure. Conversely, if your funding requirements are small, your probability of success is high, and you come up dry with all of your other possible sources, don't overlook the SBA micro-loan program. These loans are for amounts up to $35,000. See *www.sba.gov*.

Do not overlook special government programs you may qualify for—if you are a woman or ethnic minority, for example.

These programs include loans with lower interest rates and, in some cases, possibly even grants with no payback requirement. In addition to the federal government, you should look into your home state to see if they offer similar programs.

The old saying is that banks only lend money to people who have money. To an extent, this is true. But that doesn't necessarily mean your own money. If you are able to raise some of the capital you require for your start-up through friends, family, or other private individuals, you may then succeed in attracting additional bank financing. Although they are a dying breed in the face of the many bank mergers and acquisitions, we found a small, local community bank to be friendly in providing a small line of credit, once we had established a customer base and had business on the books with future receivables. For the most part, however, banks will probably rank second to last on the list for financing most start-ups. The trick is to establish a banking relationship with an institution first, whether it involves your personal or your business transactions. Demonstrate how solid and trustworthy, how prompt a payer, how valuable a customer you are. Get to know your bankers personally. Support the charities they support. Raise your stock with them by referring other worthy customers to them. Then, share your well-thought-out business plans with them. By taking the right steps, they will probably invite you to apply for a loan. Do everything you possibly can to lower their risk and exposure. Most of all, practice full disclosure; do not leave any unexpected or unexplained surprises.

Character counts. As much as it would appear to be a numbers game, bankers have a coveted place and an image to maintain within the community. Michael A. Russo, who spent some thirty years at both large and small institutions, recalls an incident when he served as a loan officer. His boss sent him out to see a video rental store that had applied for a loan. Unbeknownst to him, it turned out the applicant operated a XXX pornography shop. Russo flatly refused to approve the loan application, in spite of his boss's urging.

Omar would agree, citing the five Cs that lenders look for:

- **Capacity:** the ability to repay the debt (cash flow)
- **Capital:** the owner's own investment (skin in the game)
- **Collateral:** assets, real estate, equipment
- **Conditions:** industry trends for your business
- **Character:** your background, resume, and credibility

Banks go in cycles: for a period, they loosen lending standards; then, as the nonperforming (slow-paying or nonpaying) loans mount up, they once again tighten up their standards. During the affluent 1980s, banks loosened up business credit requirements. It came back to bite them.

A client of Barry's bought land on speculation, selling the parcels to builders. He engaged in a dangerous game of leveraging one piece of property against another—borrowing against one parcel to buy the next one. As long as the demand existed and he found a buyer, it posed no problems. Eventually, the bust came. Homebuyers stopped buying; homebuilders stopped building; the builders stopped buying land; he could no longer pay the bank notes and the banks foreclosed, selling off the land at sacrifice prices. Then, the bankers tightened the screws on the lending machine.

Ultimately, bankers are a conservative lot by nature. They operate in a risk-averse manner. When they see red flags, they back off. What are some of the danger signs that scare them off? Questionable credit history, previous bankruptcy, lack of prior experience in business, lack of collateral, and questionable character will all send your friendly banker running for cover. Hint: If your own personal balance sheet looks weak, consider bringing in others with greater financial strength, even if only in an advisory capacity. Offer them at least a small share of ownership (equity), even if they are nonvoting shares.

Debt or Equity: Which Is Right for You?

Equity refers to giving up a portion of your ownership in return for funding, typically by selling shares in your company. The downsides to this arrangement: you lose both control while you are operating the business and value when you go to sell the enterprise. According to Omar, equity financing works best if the equity partner has strengths to complement your weaknesses.

Debt, of course, refers to borrowing money. Obviously, maintaining control is the upside of debt financing. Omar remarks, "In today's low interest environment, borrowed money makes sense. You have the flexibility to pay off the loan; it's harder to buy out a partner. The downside: People with poor credit won't be able to attract financing."

Some entrepreneurs are able to work a combination of debt and equity financing to launch their start-ups. In either case, you need a strong business concept to attract lenders or investors.

SMART-START TIP

Shore Up Your Balance Sheet

Add weight to your financial statements before you approach bankers. Bring in minority shareholders with higher net worth to to attract debt and to give credibility to your financial position.

Become a Funding Magnet

Omar places a great deal of weight on having a well-written business plan. So, what does that look like? "One that substantiates the promises, projections, and assumptions you make. It should be comprehensive, with testimonials and references from credible people that know you. It should be well researched, with trends for your industry, copies of tax returns, and the credentials of a good team—an accountant, a business advisor, and an attorney. Coming up with less collateral requires you to do a better job of telling your story. The worst thing is a canned business plan with no personality or spirit."

Omar gives the example of his client, a company manufacturing equipment for hazardous materials testing. The group attracted a substantial line of credit. Why? They were highly credentialed in their field; they had a niche with a growth trajectory; they exhibited the five Cs; the owner had invested his own capital and presented a customized plan in a series of in-person meetings.

We have seen entrepreneurs spend so much time raising money that they will miss their window of opportunity to lead the market. In more than one case, a less ambitious, scaled-down plan might have attracted financing sooner. If your business concept involves a new technology or discovery that is not entirely proprietary, this could apply to you. So, what are realistic expectations for a start-up seeking financing? Omar recommends:

- Financing will be more difficult to get if it is unsecured
- It will take a lot of persistence, knocking on doors
- You should have a timeline
- You should have a Plan B (less grandiose)

Over the years, while helping our clients write and shop their business plans, we have noted the most frequent reasons start-ups fail to attract funding. We have seen some of the most promising products shelved for these reasons. They are:

- **One-Product Companies**—No matter how breakthrough the technology or invention, many lenders and investors will not fund a business with a single revenue stream.

Why? A larger competitor can easily trample your enterprise; the product may become obsolete.

- **No Track Record of Sales**—At this point, you have a possibly spectacular idea. However, it has not withstood the test of the marketplace. Conducting at least some informal market research may at least validate interest and demand.
- **Inadequate Management Team**—You may be an outstanding inventor or product developer, but running a business demands many other skill sets you simply don't have. If your potential investors are venture capitalists, you run the risk of them gaining excessive control of your enterprise under the guise of putting a proper team in place. Protect yourself by lining up a highly experienced team in the key critical areas of finance, human resources, sales, and marketing. Indicate your intention to hire the team when the funding is in place.

The key involves setting up the proper formula to repay your investors and retain control of your enterprise. When possible, Limited Partnerships have a great win-win potential for both the investor and the entrepreneur. This arrangement spells out a relatively high rate of return after a specified period of time. Once the investors receive their payout, their shares may revert back to the business owner. Building contractors and film producers have used this arrangement to their advantage, with each new project set up as a separate company. This protects the assets of the other business entities against any negative consequences—lawsuits, insurance claims, etc.

LOCK AND LOAD YOUR BUSINESS PLAN

We have two mirrors in this book—one where you reflect and one where the experts reflect on their experience. Look into the second mirror, on the opposite wall.

We asked Andy Bello, senior managing director at Global Arena Capital, an investment banking firm in New York City, to reflect on how to ensure your business plan. Bello has financed deals of all sizes for start-ups and early stage companies in the United States and overseas, and has great advice for Smart-Starts. The three biggest mistakes entrepreneurs typically make when they seek financing are:

- Underestimate the amount of money they actually need
- Paint an overly optimistic picture of how well they will do
- Fail to think through a solid business plan

So, what does Bello recommend you do to remedy these mistakes?

- Especially if it's your first time raising money, speak to as many people as you can who have been on your side of the table.
- Speak to people who have already been through the process of raising money.
- Solicit advice from bankers and financiers.

Andy compares the role of a good investment banker to a film company. The investment banker serves as the director; the business plan is the script; and the cast is the management team for your business. Good investment bankers can and will introduce you to the people who can help you.

Private Placements

Private investment can come in the form of close friends and family, or if you need to raise a substantial sum, it may take the form of a private placement. Private placements are regulated by the Securities and Exchange Commission, since the number of investors approached is often much larger. Private placements often involve institutional investors as well as private individuals. These are large groups of people approached by investment bankers. Although the investors are aware of the often higher risk potential, the Private Placement Memorandum (PPM) requires detailed disclosures. The return promised generally exceeds the percentages paid by more traditional investments like stocks and bonds, treasury notes, and certificates of deposit. In order to avoid abuses, the regulators require these investors to certify that they have a substantial net worth and that their participation in a private placement is strictly risk capital they can afford to lose. Generally, these individuals invest a minimum of significant units, ranging from $5,000–$10,000 to $100,000 units or more.

Private Placements: The Components

In almost every situation where you will need to raise outside funding for your venture, the instrument you will use is what is known as a Private Placement Memorandum, commonly referred to as a PPM. Whether you are raising $50,000 or $5 million, you will need a legal document that answers your potential investors' several basic questions:

- What is your business?
- What is the deal?
- What is the form of security I will receive?
- What are the risks?
- What is the price I will be paying per share or per unit and what does that get me as a percentage of ownership?

35

Since private placements are legal documents with complex rules, we strongly suggest that you don't try this yourself without the help of an experienced securities attorney. On the other hand, however, PPMs aren't mystical or even particularly complex documents. Much of the work to create them can be done by you to help reduce your costs and accelerate your ability to get into fundraising mode. To give you an idea of the components of a typical PPM and those sections you can work on yourself and the ones that will need to be done by your attorney, we give you the following list:

Business Description
This section of the PPM contains much of the material that would be contained in your business plan, but in an abbreviated form. Also, because this is a legal document, the business description is written in a factual tone and is less of a marketing presentation of your business than might be found in your business plan.

Transaction Summary
In this relatively short section of the PPM, you declare how much money you are raising, the form of security you are offering (common shares, preferred shares), and how much of the total company will be acquired for the investment. In this section, it is often common to include a Use of Proceeds section that describes how the investment will be used (to expand marketing, to build inventory, to maintain operations).

Blue Sky Warnings
This is a state-by-state listing of specific requirements or limitations that may apply. If you are raising money from investors who may reside in states other than the one in which you reside, you will need to include these sections. This section is highly technical, and should be the responsibility of your attorney.

Lists of Risks

This is a section that should be compiled by both you and your attorney. Your attorney will want to make this section much longer and more exhaustive than you will think reasonable. In this section you will list all the possible ways in which your business could fail and investors could lose their money. Most entrepreneurs look at the risk section as deal killers, but just stay calm, as difficult as it may be. Take a deep breath and work co-operatively with your attorney here. This section is necessary as a legal protection, and all sophisticated investors are used to looking at these sections for what they are—a necessary part of a legal document. And by the way, really asking yourself about ways your business could fail can give you ways to protect yourself against those unlikely but possible situations.

Financial Projections and Assumptions

Typically these can be done as appendices, but it is important they are done in sufficient detail so that investors can reasonably understand the economics of your business. Often, the assumptions to the financial projections, which are written as a narrative, can be as important as the financials themselves, in that they show how carefully you've thought about your business. In the financial projections, you will need profit and loss projections, balance sheet projections, and cash flow projections. The amount of detail you provide will depend on how big your business is projected to be and how much funding you are seeking. Typically, you will need to provide projections for three to five years.

Description of the Security

This is where you describe the form of security you are offering: shares of stock, debt, a convertible note. Again, it is advisable to work with competent start-up attorneys or investment advisors when determining the best form of security you can offer. Each has its own benefits and disadvantages and the one you choose depends on a number of factors, not least of which is how fast you believe you can achieve cash flow.

Accredited Investor Documents

If you are raising money from individuals rather than from a venture fund, you will need to attach documents that can be completed by the investors that show they are accredited. This means they have certification that they meet certain annual income or net worth requirements. The goal here is to ensure that you are not raising money from people who are naive or who would be materially damaged by a loss in this investment.

A Guide to Acquiring Funding

If your business start up requires more capital than you can raise by yourself, from banks, or from small business loans, you have to access funding from other people. There are pros and cons to this. First, you are now moving into a world where your own personal capital will no longer be the limiting factor to your growth. Secondly, you are diversifying your own personal risk—not all of the money invested in your start-up is yours. And if you value your sleep, that can be a big factor. Thirdly, if you pick the right investors they can bring more than money—they can bring knowledge, contacts, ways to accelerate your growth, and emotional and professional support. We strongly recommend, by the way, finding funding partners who have the willingness to help you grow as well as provide the money. Additionally, depending on the level of professionalism of the funders you find, they can bring legal, accounting, and other resources to your venture.

And this is where the negatives come in: now you are not alone. And when you accept other people's money, you do give up some ownership and control. The amount of both depends on a number of factors, including the sources from whom you gain the funding. In order of accessibility, you can raise funds from family and friends (by the way, everyone will tell you to go to these people first), then so-called angel funders, investment banks, venture funds, and institutional funders.

Family and Friends

Being an entrepreneur can be a great way to find every true friend you have ever had. It is also a good way to learn humility. Because the very first amount of money you will likely raise for your venture, whether it is to fund your market research or the development of products or your business concept, will have to come before you have a viable business plan. This is what is known as true seed capital and prior to the dot.com bust, it was often provided by venture funds. No longer. To find seed money you will typically need to go to family and friends who believe in you and your ideas. Treat them well, for they are truly investing in you.

SMART-START TIP

Don't Win at Business and Lose Everything Else

One of the key issues in doing a start-up is the tradeoffs we are often required to make. To create something from nothing takes a huge act of will and incredible commitments of time, passion, and personal energy. As the business develops it can become all-consuming, to the exclusion of family, friends, church, and other organizations that add value and perspective to life. Don't win at business and destroy every other aspect of your life. We strongly recommend you try to find balance in a regular and ritualistic way — for example, making time for a family dinner every night before going back to work. It may be hard at first, but we know for sure that you will be refreshed, perform better, and have a better relationship with your family if you make sure to carve out time for them.

Angel Investors and Angel Groups

After family and friends come angel investors. These angels are typically affluent individuals with disposable income and an interest to get higher rewards for higher-risk investments. They also know they may lose some or all of their investment. Often these angels are affluent professionals, doctors, lawyers, accountants, or business owners who have disposable funds to invest. Typically, these angels make investments in the range of $5,000–$25,000 per investor. Sometimes you can find "whales" who may be able to invest in the $100,000 or more range. After the dot.com bust, the role of true venture funders was abandoned by venture capital funds and picked up by these angel funders. Angel investors have provided the capital that just wouldn't be available anywhere else for even the best business concepts as venture funds lick their wounds and seek second-stage or mezzanine funding opportunities only.

Almost every major city, and many smaller cities as well, will have formal or informal angel networks or groups. These groups often hold formal presentation meetings where you can address 20 to 100 potential investors at a time. The groups are a collection of individuals, each of whom will make their own investment decision, but they are a great way to access a large number of people at one time, all of whom are at least interested in seed investing.

Investment Banks

If your business has significant revenue potential or your strategy calls for the acquisition of other businesses, investment banks may be appropriate fund-raising partners. You should understand, however, that there will typically be up-front fees involved as they help prepare financing documents, business plans, and PPMs to raise money for you. Think of investment bankers as acquiring an agent in sports or book publishing. They have financial contacts, they are respected endorsers, and the fact that you are being presented by an investment bank gives you credibility with institutional funders that you would typically not have by yourself.

But understand a couple of important points. One, investment banks are not venture funders; they don't typically invest their own money, they help you raise it. Two, while having an investment bank take your project is an extremely positive step, there is no guarantee they can raise money for you. Their work is almost always done on a best-effort basis. Still, investment banks raise money for a living, and typically, entrepreneurs do not. They know the tricks of the trade here, and if they believe in you and your business model, you have a big leg up in raising the kind of serious money your business may need. Thirdly, in addition to the upfront, generally modest fees, investment banks make their serious money by generating success fees, a percentage of the money they raise. Typically this percentage ranges from 6 percent to 10 percent depending on the amount of the money raised.

You may think the success percentage model is expensive. Another way to perceive it is that you have just acquired a partner whose real compensation is directly tied in to raising the money you need. The success fees are paid out of the money they raise, and if you think of this as a sales commission, it is highly reasonable given the acceleration the funds they raise may give your business.

Investment banks are also appropriate if you are in a position to build a business based on acquiring already existing businesses. In this case, if you have a strong business plan and the appropriate experience, the investment bank may not only find businesses for you to acquire, they can also help you raise the money to acquire them. Working with an investment bank can help you deal with venture funds and institutional funders and give you the professional support that can make those interactions possible at all.

Venture Funds

Venture funds are not what they used to be. There was a time when venture funds did what their name implies—provide venture capital to start-up companies. The nineties craze for the Internet created a feeding and funding frenzy that has changed the world of venture capital ever since.

In the nineties, *Wired* magazine reported that the world of business had changed forever, and that things like profitability were the wrong metrics. Instead, it was all about growing fast and "clicks" and "unique visitors" to your website were used as replacements for dollars and cents. Well, the world of business has changed back. Profit and traditional business metrics are more important than ever, but the openness for venture funds to invest in risk has been reduced dramatically. The pendulum has swung from wild exuberance to deep conservatism. Whereas in the past you could approach a VC with a good business plan and management team and expect to receive seed funding, now many if not most venture funds are only interested in companies at the mezzanine level, that is, after they have operating revenues and profits of some significance.

While it is true that with a proprietary technology and a proven management team venture funding for true start-ups can be gained, many venture funds now require almost the same standards that banks did for funding a business. Because this is so, there is a ton of money available, and the reason is many funds are just sitting on their money, waiting for perfect deals. In fact, things have gotten so bad in this regard that a number of venture funds have closed down because they could not find enough investments that met their criteria. This is a sad thing, indeed, when venture funds only want deals that are so risk free that banks will fund them (and at better terms).

Now, it is true that some smaller or specialized venture funds remain that focus on early-stage (the stage right after seed) investments, but there's a catch here, as well. For many of these VCs the focus of investment is extremely limited. One group we know will provide early-stage funding, but they fund only businesses that produce consumer-oriented medical hardware devices.

Strategic Investors

If you are developing a product or service that can add value to an existing company's product line, you may be able to find investment funding from this company. Many large companies have their own venture groups who specifically look at investments that can accelerate the growth of their firm. When Michael was helping to launch the first video digitizer for the Apple Macintosh, the first place he went for funding was to the venture arm of Apple Computer. The video-digitizer was a product that complemented Apple's desktop publishing positioning, and there was significant interest from Apple and other Apple suppliers. The company ultimately raised money from traditional angels, but strategic partner funding has many benefits: You not only get money, you get a "big brother" who can help you succeed.

Valuing Your Company for Early Stage Funding

As we said earlier, once you access other people's money, many things change in your entrepreneurial world. The most dramatic and most inevitable is that you no longer own all of your company. Whether you find your OPM from friends and family, angels, VCs, or strategic partners, the ultimate question you will have to address for all of these is, "How much do I get for my money?" In other words, "What's the deal?"

Here's where life gets truly interesting, because what your investors get depends on the value you can get them to put on your company. In a very simple example, but not unlike what actually occurs in these negotiations, let's say you put a value on your firm of $1 million. If you are raising $100,000 in seed capital, on a valuation of $1 million dollars, the investors' ownership would be 10 percent. If you are issuing 1 million shares, let's say at $1 per share, your investors would receive 100,000 shares of the stock in your company. Your goal and the goal of your investors is to make sure that the value of your company and those shares go up over time so that your investors generate a return on their investment (ROI) that is sufficient to justify their risk.

Now, while great business schools like the University of Chicago have pioneered complex financing models to price stocks adjusted for risk, using terms like the stock's beta, none of those theoretical models typically apply for start-up ventures. Instead, in the start up world, you show the investors financial projections that indicate the stock they own will generate a ten times return on their investment. No angel investors or VCs believe you will generate a ten times return. They will automatically cut that projection in half, generating for themselves a five times return. Five hundred percent over five years—yes, that would justify the risk; in fact, so would 150%. But don't show them that, because this is a ritualistic dance in which the correct way to play is to provide numbers that other people can cut in half or by 75 percent and still generate the ROI they require. What about showing them conservative projections? To a bank, yes; for a Small Business Administration loan, yes. But if you want to raise funding based on nothing more than a business plan and a concept—the riskiest possible investment—then venture investors will want truly extraordinary returns.

Going back to our $100,000 investment in a $1 million valued company for 10 percent example: To generate a ten times ROI, the company would have to be worth $10 million so that 10 percent would be worth $1 million. Let's say, however, your investor doesn't believe you can grow that fast. They will still want a ten times ROI. They might suggest that although they love your concept, they believe it will only be worth $5 million in five years. They still need a $1 million return. A possible solution: They will want 20 percent of your company instead of 10 percent. This is where negotiation, salesmanship, and your ability to convince investors in the certainty of their return will all come into play, as you try to keep as much ownership as you can. This is a dance that invariably occurs, and you shouldn't be offended by what you may see as an investor's effort to gain the best deal they can. After all, they are the ones putting money at risk.

Eight Reasons Entrepreneurs Don't Get the Money They Need

Since for many start-ups gaining at least some amount of outside investment is critical it is important to look at the key reasons you might fail at getting the funding you need. Bryan Emerson, president of Starlight Investments (*www.starlightinvestments.com*), a nationwide firm that specializes in raising money for early stage ventures, has extensive experience in helping people find the money they need. He has identified a short list of common barriers to funding. Emerson's firm is unusual in that they focus on earlier stage companies than most investment groups, and that it is made up of twenty individual reps who are highly entrepreneurial themselves. They have a unique investor database of more than 50,000 investors, ranging from high net-worth individuals to institutional investors. Last year they raised more than $100 million for their clients, and Emerson's list of potential barriers to investment is one you should take seriously. Here's what he thinks sabotages most funding efforts:

Lack of Compelling Story
The most important thing Emerson observes is that you have to have a compelling, convincing story on how and why your start-up will succeed. Additionally, you need to be able to communicate that story in a couple of sentences—your elevator speech.

45

Lack of Clear Objectives/Goals

Amazingly, according to Emerson, the number one question that entrepreneurs fail to address is: "How much money do you need, and what valuation do you place on your company?" Bryan notes that you need to know exactly what you want, what you need it for, and the price on your stock. You need to be absolutely clear here. For example, "we need $1 million to fund us to break even, and that will get you 25 percent of the company." And you and your advisors need to have materials that support your request.

Failure to Prepare for Due Diligence

Understand that before any serious investor commits to funding your deal, they will perform a due diligence review. This will include due diligence about your personal life and background as well as about the business. If you have any personal issues or weaknesses, it is better that you present them in the best possible light than for an investor to find them independently. On the other hand, your past can be a strong reason for investing in you—if you have made money for people or other companies in the past. Your past successes can be a very powerful reason for people to invest in your next venture. Additionally, pick your references carefully and prepare them to discuss you in connection with this new venture. They need to be able to talk well not only about you, but about their belief that you will be able to succeed in this new venture.

Lack of Understanding of the Funding Process/Rules

According to Emerson, the key here is to create a win-win situation for your investors. Candid presentation of the rewards and risks in a balanced professional way is not only a way to convince investors that you are a professional they can count on, but it is also a way of avoiding shareholder lawsuits.

Reliance on Inappropriate Business Professionals

Emerson stresses that using well-respected professionals to bolster your endeavor is key. If you can attract well-known attorneys, accountants, and investment banks, it will give potential investors comfort in a couple of ways. First, it shows that the business systems aspect of your start-up will be carefully monitored and managed. Secondly, the fact that you have been able to attract quality professionals acts as at least an implied endorsement of the quality of your start-up concept, and of you as a manager.

Poor Choice of Funding Sources

As we discussed above, certain sources of funding will be more or less appropriate for your start-up idea, depending on the industry sector you compete in, the amount of funding you need, and the potential return you can predict. It is extremely common for funders to love an idea that does not fit the criteria for their investment fund. Their enthusiasm is gratifying, but don't waste time on investors who may be very attracted to your idea, but who, for example, can only invest in high-tech computer deals when you have a retail store concept. To avoid wasting time and money, try to find funding sources who invest in the type of business you have.

Not Doing Due Diligence on the Funding Source

Often, entrepreneurs are so eager to find a funder that they don't bother to research the credibility of the funders. You need to complete due diligence on your prospective funders as they complete due diligence on you. Key questions you can ask include: in what have they invested recently—what stage, what industry, what amount; what their track record is for their investors—do they make them money, are they liquid (do they have the money to invest today); how quickly they fund; and if they fund in tranches or all at once.

Being Unprepared for the Next Steps

Again, it may seem surprising, but Emerson notes that many entrepreneurs are unprepared for success in their conversations with investors. For example, after a good presentation, the investors may ask for additional documentation about the business, your formal business plan, formal financial projections, and executive summaries. You certainly don't want to derail their enthusiasm by not having these materials available immediately. They are ready to invest; don't let their interest cool or communicate that you are not as professional as you need to be by not anticipating their needs. Lastly, you will need an escrow account to accept their funding because most raises come in pieces, and cannot be acted upon until a certain percentage of the total raise is present. Your attorney or investment advisors will normally manage these escrow accounts, a "parking place" for investors' money until the determined percentage of the total funding has been attained.

SMART-START TIP

Cash Flow Changes Everything

Without positive cash flow (that is, you generate more cash than you use), your start-up has a "burn rate," the amount of money you are losing each month. If you raise $500,000 and have a burn rate of $50,000 per month, you will either have to achieve positive cash flow in ten months or be prepared to raise additional funding. When you have achieved a positive cash flow, your business is self-sustaining and you are no longer at the whims of outside funders. If you need additional funding once you have achieved positive cash flow, it is viewed as growth capital and is generally much easier to gain and gain at more positive terms than funding when you are losing money every month.

Exit Strategy: The Last Piece Must Come First

It sounds paradoxical, of course, but one of the very first things you need to do in valuing your company to raise money is to create your exit strategy. You may bridle at this concept, but think about it from an investor's perspective: Not only do investors want to know what the projected return on their investment will be, they want to know how and when they can get that return. And the choice you make about how you shape your business for exit will shape the way you can present your valuation models in raising money. If, for example, you think you may be able to take your start-up business or division public, there are multipliers that come into play that create value that is typically larger than if you just sell your business to a private party.

Passing On Your Business

One of the classic models of exiting a business is to pass it on, typically to children, spouses, or other family members. There are many ways to structure this type of exit, ranging from a gradual separation with occasional participation in the business to a formal and definite separation. This approach is most appropriate when your vision is to be an owner-operator over a long time, and when that vision is shared by other family members—hopefully representing more than one generation. This model has it risks, however, as represented by the courses in business schools that track family businesses, often titled "Rags to Riches to Rags in Three Generations." The old joke about how a third-generation owner became a millionaire—I started with $10 million and worked down—has been true enough often enough to be unfunny. Passing a business on can be a great model, however, as long as the people you intend to pass it to share your vision, passion, and business skill.

Selling Your Business

This is probably the most common exit strategy for most entrepreneurs. There are many reasons you may want to do this: you want to move on to other things, you want to cash out, you want to reward your investors, or you want to retire are among the most common of these reasons. Depending on the size of your business, this can be a fairly complex exercise, and even if you have a small business it will be wise to engage a professional to assist you in finding buyers, valuing your business, and helping with the legal issues involved. If your business is relatively small, you should consult a business broker. Whatever the size of your business, this is one area in which you absolutely should engage a professional's help. There are many ways to value a business, including multiples of revenue, multiples of EBITDA (Earnings Before Interest Taxes Depreciation Amortization, one indicator of profit), or multiples of cash flow.

SMART-START TIP

Don't Try This at Home

You have spent years building your business; spend the money and time to find a competent professional who can help you get all the value you deserve for it. Valuing a business, and selling it are complex skills; ultimately it will be a very subjective negotiation with the buyer. There are reasons professional athletes have agents — they let someone else maximize the value of their business worth. You should do the same.

Franchising Your Business

We've already talked about how franchising can be a great way to raise money for business expansion. It can also be a way to have your cake and eat it, too. One model that we have seen work for numerous entrepreneurs is to build their franchise business to multiple units, run them, and then when appropriate, sell off some or most of the franchise units. For example, one of our acquaintances owned 100 McDonald's, ran them successfully, and then gradually sold most of them off, generating real wealth for his investors and himself. He still owns a couple of units—a number that he can manage without stress.

Public Offerings

The words, "I'm going public" used to be the Valhalla of any entrepreneur. The stories of garage start-ups going public and turning their founders into millionaires is the stuff of entrepreneurial daydreams. And while going public is still a viable and profitable option for certain types of companies, it is certainly less viable and less attractive than it once was for many types of companies. Again, this has much to do with the dot.com bust, in which the goal for virtually every venture-funded start-up was to go public quickly, reap a handsome reward, and for many, get out. Many entrepreneurs in the nineties were less interested in building successful businesses than in doing the things necessary to get their company public—and their venture-funding partners were strong accomplices in this. Even for sincere and highly professional executives who wanted to build real businesses, the hype and pressure and unrealistic expectations of the stock market made it impossible to create truly viable ongoing businesses.

One of our good friends was the CFO of a dot.com that grew at a fabulous rate—from $0 to $50 million in five years. In a normal world, that would be growth of which to be proud. Except that the hyper-inflated dot.com stock market had given the company a market valuation of over $1 billion when they had revenues of less than $10 million per year. No matter how successful they were, the market had already inflated their stock price to a level that could never be achieved in the real world.

As a reaction to this public-offering mania, it is typically more difficult to go public in a serious way than most people think. In addition, because of the issues that surrounded the Enron collapse and other major company scandals, regulations surrounding public companies have been greatly tightened and made more complex and orders of magnitude more expensive. Chief among these expense generators is the Sarbanes-Oxley laws, which affect the relationship between accounting firms and their clients. The good news is that there can be a significant multiplier attached to the value of your company if you are a fast-growing firm or one with a "sexy" story that the market embraces. If you build a company with revenues and profits that can support the costs of being public, there can be real rewards in going public. It's just more difficult and somewhat less fun than it used to be.

Acquisition by a Strategic Partner

If going public was the sexy exit strategy of the past, the new sexy exit strategy is being acquired by a large strategic partner. Faster, easier, and potentially more lucrative than going public, strategic acquisition has made billionaires of the guys who founded MySpace, Facebook, and a variety of lesser known companies. The concept here is that large companies like Google or Microsoft, for example, can pay a ridiculously large price for a company that has small sales, but which has the potential to add value to the acquirers' sales and, even more importantly, its stock price. Think about it this way: Let's say there is a large public company with revenues of $2 billion and 300,000 shares outstanding. Let's also say they can acquire a small start-up that allows them to compete in a new market. Having a new story for the financial markets excites the analysts, and they raise the price of the large acquiring firm a small amount—say $1 per share. That's an increase in market valuation of $300 million. Paying an inflated price to the small start-up that adds that value can make great economic sense. If the start-up has real potential for growth, especially under the wings of its new acquirer, that stock impact can grow even larger over time. And for the acquired company, life just got much better: a huge financial return, no costs of going public, no issues with Sarbanes-Oxley—the acquiring company does all of that. It's a great story, and a great strategy. You just need to find a business that complements or answers a real problem for a large existing firm. As you think about your start-up, you just might want to have this strategy in the back of your mind, because it is the brass ring of current entrepreneurial exits.

Smart-Start Summary: Keys to Attracting Your Funding

1. No matter what the amount, investors need to know how soon you can achieve profitability.
2. Weigh the advantages of a cash infusion against giving up a share of ownership and control.
3. Don't do this alone; get professional help raising funds.
4. When you are raising money, think like an investor. Investors want to know the following about the return they will receive on their investment: How large? How certain? When?

4

Build a Smart-Start Company Structure

Of all the things that confuse entrepreneurs, issues about structuring their business probably head the list. There are good reasons for this, since these are relatively technical and legal issues and most entrepreneurs are not only not familiar with issues about company structure, they're intimidated by them. We've all heard terms like C-corp, partnership, and LLC (Limited Liability Corporation), but few of us understand what the difference is among these entities and why to choose one corporate structure versus another.

Choosing the right structure is important for a variety of reasons. All of these structures give you protections legally and financially and will be important as tools in helping you attract and raise capital. The right structure can also be important in allowing you to pursue the exit strategy you may prefer. For example, if you plan on taking your company public at some point, you will have to choose a specific type of corporate structure. If you plan to own and operate your company, there will be significant benefits from other types of company structures.

While there are highly technical issues involved here, the core differences among these company structures are relatively simple and straightforward. There are three reasons you shouldn't lose sleep over corporate structure.

You Can Change Your Company Structure

This simple fact is emphasized in our conversations with Bill Walker, a former Securities and Exchange Commission attorney and advisor to numerous start-ups. Walker is a calming figure who takes the entrepreneurial perspective to legal matters. He says, "What most entrepreneurs never hear is that they should relax about corporate structure, because they can change it relatively easily. A firm that starts out as a partnership or an LLC can become a corporation, if it makes sense. An S-Corp can become a C-Corp even more easily. It all depends on what the goals of the business are and if those goals are changing, so, too, can your structure."

It's Easier to Create a Legal Structure Than Ever Before

One of the great surprises for many entrepreneurs who we work with is how easy and inexpensive it is to legally incorporate or create a partnership. Here's a quick quiz that can emphasize these points:

1. To legally incorporate in most states it will cost:
   a. $5,000–$10,000
   b. $1,000–$2,000
   c. $2,500–$5,000
   d. $200–$500

If you picked "d," $200–$500, you are right—but, we bet, somewhat surprised, too.

2. To legally incorporate in most states it will take:
   a. One to two months
   b. One to two weeks
   c. Three to six months
   d. Thirty minutes to an hour

Again, you are probably getting the idea that "d," thirty minutes to an hour, the surprisingly short answer, is correct.

You may be scratching your head and saying these numbers sound too good to be true. That you can be incorporated in thirty to sixty minutes and that all it will cost is a couple of hundred dollars is certainly not what expensive lawyers would like you to know. But because of the Internet, availability of Internet forms directly from your Secretary of State's office, and the speed of the Internet, all of these facts are now true. Another great alternative is to use an Internet firm like LegalZoom.com. Using LegalZoom is extremely simple and clear. They take you through an incorporation in a foolproof way. And it costs hundreds of dollars—not thousands. We use LegalZoom all the time, because they offer a one-stop service that goes beyond even what you get from the secretary of state. Paying a high-priced lawyer who uses her own forms not only costs more and takes more time, it bogs things down for the administrators at the Secretary of State's office.

Sure, IBM will always use its own lawyers; but you are a start-up, not a large company. And this is one place where it would be a mistake to spend too much money on something the government, or the Internet, facilitates so well. This is one of those rare situations where cutting out the middleman is not only more efficient, and less expensive, it may even be better legally.

There Are Plenty of Competent Advisors to Help

While we advise going to LegalZoom or your state's Secretary of State website and reviewing their forms for incorporating your firm or creating a partnership or Limited Liability Corporation to see just how simple this process can be, some of you will want to talk with someone in person about your corporate structure decisions. There's good news here as well. In almost every major city there are nonprofit start-up advisory groups happy to help you review your business plan and strategy and help you choose the right structure. They will even help you walk through the incorporation process and can take you to the Secretary of State website and talk you through the process.

A good example of this is the Houston Technology Center. The HTC exists to help entrepreneurs, and they have reference materials as well as advisors who can really help you with many of the more technical issues surrounding your business start-up. Whatever form of corporate structure you choose protects you legally and financially. Review your choices, get advice, and create that structure before you actively begin any activities. The actual work of creating that structure and incorporating or creating a partnership is much easier, faster, and less expensive than it ever has been.

Company Structure as a Smart-Start Policy

Today, when it comes to business formation, it's not a good idea to be a sole proprietor; your personal assets are at risk. DBA or "doing business as" trade names make you personally liable. Attorney Mitch Beinhaker (*www.mcbesq.com*) recommends an LLC or Limited Liability Corporation. These are partnership-like entities that give you corporate protection. You can have a one-person LLC in many states. For a minimal fee in most states, you can go to the state's websites and file to create your LLC online. Beinhaker cautions, "You must sign everything as an LLC officer; set up bank accounts in the name of the LLC; don't pay the company's bills out of your personal accounts." Otherwise, he cautions, if there is ever a question of personal versus corporate liability, you will have difficulty maintaining the protection. A claimant can then pierce the corporate veil and attempt to hold you personally liable and go after your personal assets. Next, get a certificate of incorporation from the state. You can even get a Federal Tax ID Number from the IRS online. The beauty of it all is that you can set up an LLC within minutes!

Now that you've protected your personal assets by incorporating your business, you still need to protect your company's assets by insuring properly. You should have a business owner's policy with $500,000 or more in protection. Plus, you should have liability insurance on your homeowner's policy. Beinhaker advises, "Having the insurance makes it more likely that you can settle the claim."

Now that you have a proper business structure, get all of your customer agreements in writing. Your invoice or bill of sale should state your terms. Professional services firms should have a written agreement. Even contractor's estimates should be in writing. Have agreements reviewed by an attorney. If you're two people or more in business together, at least have a letter of intent at the time you start up, if not a formal operating agreement. Properly drafted agreements can protect partners against ex-spouses, widows, etc. Formulate your agreements when everyone is getting along; it's too hard later.

Beinhaker counsels start-ups to have a relationship with an attorney that can create an enforceable agreement clearly spelling out your liability. It should also spell out if there are changes. For example, if you deal with homeowners, many states have consumer fraud acts. Violations can result in treble damages, which are often statutory—the judge has no discretion.

What about when you, the business owner, become the customer? You must have someone who can review your vendors' contracts and interpret them for you. For example, if you rent space, when it comes to commercial leases—both office and retail—everything is negotiable. Always read what you sign.

If you're buying a business, don't do it on your own. Beinhaker suggests, when possible, to buy the assets of the business. That way, you won't incur the liabilities that may come down the road. Here's an example: A lawsuit is filed after you buy the business by someone who claims to have slipped and fallen on the business property. If you bought the assets but not the business itself, you would not be a party to that lawsuit.

When you begin hiring employees, Beinhaker advises, have a good accountant or payroll company, first and foremost. If you are an at-will state, you must notify employees of the fact that their employment can be terminated at any time. Be careful of letting them go if they are members of a minority or pregnant.

Document poor performance. Some people will prey on discrimination and liability issues.

Beinhaker's advice to the start-up:

- Set yourself up properly
- Set up your company, get insurance, and get the proper documents
- When your business becomes viable, be concerned with death and disability
- If you are a sole proprietor, determine how you will eventually walk away
- Agreements should prevent bringing in outside partners

Business continues to change. How is it different today from in the past and what should we expect in the future? Beinhaker admits it's easier today to form a business, and technology has made it faster. At the same time, it's more difficult in another way. We operate in a more litigious society, so we need more liability protection than before. Claims can be filed against you and they can find more information out about you in the information age.

Some jurisdictions offer more protection than others. For example, a Nevada corporation makes your assets more inaccessible—they're not listed under your tax ID number. This can apply if you have assets in excess of $10 million or if you are in a profession subject to high liability exposure. In some cases, creating a foreign entity may also prove beneficial. For example, Beinhaker advises offshore LLCs would provide limited access to your company's assets. Another strategy, known as a Series LLC, often applies to firms with intellectual property or real estate. This involves setting up different business units for each project, protecting each one.

In short, a solid business plan and the right structure from the outset help you focus on all of the most critical aspects of launching your start-up, helps you plan for the future growth and development of your business from the outset, and helps convince your potential suppliers, funding partners, and advisors that your business has a high likelihood of success.

Building Your Personal Partnerships

Where should I look for partners and how do I know they will make good partners?

Today, you have advantages in your favor when you're checking people out. So, let's talk about where to look for partners first; then, we'll talk about how to check them out. Start with people you know you can trust, that can recommend people who are qualified. Like those retired guys from the industry you intend to go into and people who supply that industry. Go to your accountant, your lawyer, your banker; ask them who they know. Ask highly credible people for referrals to highly qualified people.

When you find them, you've got to feel them out and see if they have any interest. You've got to convince them you've got a good business idea, and you've got to get them to feel comfortable with you, too. You've got to check them out—you've got to get some references on these people. Then get references on the references, do a little research. Go on the Internet, do a little background checking, get some intelligence on them. The point is you can't just take anybody's word for anything; too many people have been duped.

You want a partner who knows things you don't know, right? So, look for someone who has complementary skill sets to your own. Suppose you're kind of nerdy—probably good with computers, right? Okay with finances, too? So, get somebody who's gotten his hands a little dirty, a nuts-and-bolts operations kind of guy. Get someone who's more of a people person than you are.

Let's broaden the definition of partner for the purposes of this discussion. It's just as important to find good companies—

and companies are only as good as the people in them—to supply you with products or services as it is to find partners inside of your business. You see, if you're really going to succeed at this business, you need those suppliers to act like partners. You've got to do the same thing when you look for suppliers. Yes, go out and interview them, just as if you were hiring them. Then, get references and do research on them so you can increase the likelihood that they will come through for you.

Here are some sources for checking out suppliers:

www.Hoovers.com—It could cost you, but it could be worth it to find out how solid the company's revenues are.

www.dnb.com—Dun & Bradstreet reports may have lost their glow, to some extent. The company operates on a pay-to-play basis—detailed information only appears on those companies that pay D&B. In addition, many companies do not report to them. Therefore, the credit ratings in the database are often incomplete.

Standard & Poor's, Moody's, and Dow Jones are excellent sources, but they only track publicly traded companies. Look for trade associations in the Encyclopedia of Associations for your supplier's industry. Ask them for any positive or negative information on the companies you plan to use. If your supplier is in a regulated industry, there is generally more information available. For example, insurance companies are rated by agencies like A.M. Best; banks, insurers, securities dealers, and other financial service providers answer to both federal and state authorities, such as the Securities and Exchange Commission, the Federal Trade Commission, etc.

Scott Stein, vice president of Zermatt Associates, a business broker, likes to talk to the editors of trade magazines—they are knowledgeable, yet often overlooked, sources of good industry intelligence. Stein also recommends checking out *www.Trade ShowWeekly.com*. Here is another place to find the trade shows in your industry so you can attend them and meet the movers and shakers: *www.TSNN.com*.

Start-Ups: A Personal View from the Trenches

Unless you're already a serial entrepreneur and you've done this several times over, you need a roadmap to navigate the choppy waters. Just as important, you need all the advice you can get. Remember: In business, as in life, there are sins of omission and sins of commission.

If you've only worked in corporate America all of your life and you're about to embark on your own first venture, you're in for a rude awakening. So many start-ups have failed because the founders failed to make the often drastic adjustments from life in a large corporation to the rigorous demands of entrepreneurship. So what does the view look like at ground-floor level? We're there every day, so we have no problem telling you.

First and foremost, while your business takes its first baby steps, you need to hold its hand—nonstop. During the critical start-up (and even some of the early growth) phase, your business is a newborn child. It clamors for your constant attention all day, every day. Put your golf clubs away; work until the work is done; meet every deadline with dogged determination; outthink, outmaneuver, and outrun your competitors constantly. Entrepreneurship is a way of life. Prepare for it. Take short vacations—not long cruises—if you want to stay afloat.

You're not in Kansas anymore—or Wall Street. The only perks are in the coffee—and the ability to control your own destiny. Unless you have incredible luck, timing, and the product of the millennium, expect your start-up to take over most of your waking hours. Expect to make sacrifices, and clear it with your family—make sure they are onboard to make those sacrifices with you. Chances are, during the start-up phase, you won't have a lot of help or a great deal of resources. Get used to scaling back both your business and your personal lifestyles.

Overhead is the Enemy

Absent a lottery win, a settlement from a major lawsuit, or an extremely wealthy family benefactor, plan on living—and operating your business—within limited means. Even if you have major investors, getting to profitability is the goal—not spending money on overhead. A client of ours previously worked for a major financial services corporation and became accustomed to all the benefits of a generous expense account. When he started his own company he failed to change his spending patterns, even though he had virtually no personal income from his business. In time, one of his partners pulled out, along with a significant amount of the operation's funding, simply because he could not tolerate the rampant spending. After a few years in business, the company's founder had plundered his family's equity in two vacation homes along with his (inherited) principal residence. Still, the founder went ahead and leased a new vehicle every couple of years, put a hot tub in the back yard, went skiing—hopefully, you get the idea.

Let's flip the coin and look at the other side. When Barry launched his advertising and production company, we set up shop in one room of an old cinderblock building that housed a printing company. After several months, we expanded to the adjoining room as well. Our audio-visual equipment sat on old supermarket shelving donated by a friend. We bought lightly used equipment from two friends: one that was upgrading his recording studio; the other who decided to pack it in and abandon his business. While in the midst of a move to our second and larger location, we passed a doctor's office that had just been refurnished. Lo and behold, there was the desk I still use today. My partner jokingly tells people our favorite store is Curbside Office Supply. Why is this important? We certainly could have bought a desk. But furniture does not produce a return on investment. The money goes into our production equipment instead, because it helps us generate revenue by completing billable jobs for our clients. By purchasing good-quality used studio equipment that we own outright (for a fraction of the cost of new equipment), we have protected ourselves against down times. When we have little or no production workload, we don't experience a bleed.

Wear many hats. Until you generate enough revenue to pay yourself and a staff, you need to run a lean operation. The trick here is to perform as many functions as you can perform well and to know which ones to delegate—almost nobody can do everything well. Those of us who worked in small entrepreneurial environments before starting our own enterprises trained for this. During the early years of Barry's broadcast career, he worked at small, distressed radio operations. Although his principal function was advertising sales, the company had no copywriter. In a short time, Barry learned how to write copy, and he also learned how to produce commercials. When he was hired as a general manager for a turnaround, he knew what to do.

Growth Enterprises, an operator of casual theme restaurants, used this philosophy when they trained their managers. Each manager's training period involved working at every single job in the house—from washing dishes to waiting tables, from cooking to ordering food. Why did this system work so well for Growth restaurants? When any staff member called in sick, the manager could jump in and perform his job.

This brings us to another critical point. If you are an entrepreneur engaging in a small start-up, nothing is beneath you. When Barry managed the distressed radio station, during the turnaround, he had extremely limited resources. He recruited, hired, and trained advertising salespeople, conducted ad hoc audience research, devised and executed station promotions and publicity, sold and serviced new and existing advertising accounts, collected accounts receivable, wrote and produced commercials—and yes, cleaned the office.

When you treat your operation like your life depends upon it—because it does—you prepare yourself for the lean years, and rest assured, there will be lean years. By learning to live within the means of your business, you protect yourself against your entrepreneurial enemies: the rising costs of your overhead, the increasing number of competitors, the price sensitivity of the marketplace—in short, all of the forces that erode your profit margins.

If you have followed this Smart-Start approach and contained your costs, held off unnecessary purchases, and kept a lean start-up staff, you have prepared yourself for controlled growth. You and your team must decide when a move to larger quarters, the addition of staff, or the purchase of equipment will actually produce a justifiable return on those investments. By not becoming overextended, you have retained the resources you will need for the next phase in the growth of your start-up. Leaving enough available credit and managing your credit lines well can make the difference between leaping to the next step or dying on the vine.

So, those of us who have done our time in the trenches advise you to carry these keys to success and plug them in to ignite your enterprise:

- **Think like** a bean counter (that's an accountant to you) when you open your checkbook.
- **Think like** a marketer when you write your business plan and design your enterprise.
- **Think like** a guerilla warrior when you enter the marketplace.
- **Think like** a therapist when you manage your staff.

◆ **Think like** a clergyman when you engage in customer service.

No matter what you do, always lead by example. Always under-promise and over-deliver; never the reverse. Let nothing but your family, your health, and your faith come between you and your business—and we mean nothing. My friend George the Greek, an independent filmmaker, waited tables and financed his films with his own personal credit cards. Every time a new girlfriend came into his life, he gave her the same warning: "Sweetheart, I can only give you one, maybe two nights a week. I have to work on my movies. If you're going to want more than that, then don't get involved with me." He meant it. The minute anyone tried to get him to give up more nights, he dropped her.

Be unstoppable, but be willing to be imperfect. John DiPietro, a fellow broadcast advertising professional from Boston, penned his book based on a workshop he conducts. The title should resonate with every start-up: *You Don't Have to Be Perfect to be Great.*

Smart-Start Summary: Tools for Building a Winning Company Structure

1. Consider protecting your personal and business assets when you choose the type of business entity to establish.
2. You can incorporate online with firms like legalzoom.com for hundreds of dollars and in minutes.
3. Re-evaluate and change the form of business entity if necessary.
4. Get competent legal and accounting advice—consider tax implications for each type of business entity.
5. Control your overhead during the early stages of your business.

5

Create an Augmented Product Line

As you thought about your start-up, you probably assumed that the product or products you were going to sell were obvious. Whatever your concept, the product you were going to sell was obvious to you, but your product decisions are much more complex than you might think. You might think you are selling coffee or pizza or software, but to succeed in the competitive world we now face, you have to be selling much more than a simple product.

When you think about the product at the base of your concept you need to think about what can be called the core product, the completed product, the augmented product, the differentiated product, and the testified product.

You may ask, "Can't I just sell pizza?" Not if you want to beat your competitors, who are all selling pizza and more. To illustrate this, let's look at one of the most famous examples of a company that achieved huge success through augmenting their core product, which, in this case, happened to be pizza: Domino's.

As anyone who's ever eaten a Domino's pizza will probably testify, it is not the best or tastiest pizza you have ever eaten. We all probably have a local mom and pop pizzeria that we love, and whose core product, delicious pizza, delivers on the core promise better than Domino's. Yet, Domino's is a multibillion-dollar business empire with storefronts in almost every town, nationwide.

How can this be? Because Domino's doesn't sell pizza. At least not as its primary product. What Domino's sells is convenience, and speedy guaranteed delivery. In our busy lives, we often make a tradeoff between best quality and convenience. And for Domino's, their thirty-minute delivery guarantee is valued more than better-tasting pizza that we might have to go pick up or have delivered later than we need it.

The contemporary world of product success is filled with similar stories, and if you want to protect your product you need to take a comprehensive approach to developing your product. Let's look at every piece of product development, step by step.

Core Product

Your core product is perhaps the clearest part of your start-up concept. Somehow, you've come to the idea that you can develop a cheaper, more efficient widget. Whether that product is coffee or software or insurance, there are many other decisions you will have to make before you go to market. There was a time, of course, when a product was simple—but that was in a commodity world, where there was no mass marketing and markets were local. Michael saw this change captured in history when he was visiting one of his clients, Kraft Foods. At one point, he got to see some of the earliest ads ever run by Joseph Kraft, for his cheese. Prior to Kraft, cheese was not differentiated. It was sold in general stores, at commodity prices. Joseph Kraft's first ads basically did two things—created a brand and said Kraft cheese was better. Those ads look amazingly naive and simple today, but in that world, he was the first to make any national claim, any claim at all, about a difference in his product. And of course, the world of cheese has never been the same.

Completed Product

As you think about your completed product, you will want to think about how to incorporate at least 4 Ps into your completed product equation. Those four Ps include Price, Place, Packaging, and Promotion.

Price

Price is as much a part of your completed product as any other component. For one thing, price is a major communicator of your product's value position. Being the most expensive product, for example, communicates that you should be the highest quality or the rarest. Being the least expensive product communicates you may be a great value or that you are an inferior product that could be easily replaced. Companies like Geico Insurance or E-Trade have made price a huge part of their product offering. Sure Geico sells insurance, but there is no ad they run that doesn't emphasize heavily the fact that with Geico you can save hundreds of dollars per year. E-Trade is an online securities brokerage whose product is based largely on a fixed price per trade.

Place

Place also may be a key element of your product that your customer is buying. To appreciate this, you need to broaden your concept to include aspects like geographic location, your customer's home, shelf space, and marketing placements.

Starting with the obvious, place literally can mean where you sell your product. For retail firms like McDonald's, the heavy traffic locations they target for their outlets may be as important as the quality of the food or the prices they charge. McDonald's will not open a new location without first conducting research to determine whether a new restaurant might adversely impact an existing location. They station interviewers inside the store and ask customers about their travel patterns. For one of our former clients, Service Corporation International, the world's largest funeral home company, place is the key to their product offering. For years, Service Corp. has made a practice of acquiring funeral homes with the most prestigious locations in each of the cities or towns in which they compete.

For other companies, place may be the opposite of retail locations. For Amazon.com, for example, place meant that consumers didn't have to go to a retail store—instead, they could shop in the privacy of their homes. While it is true that Amazon also offered lower prices, the fact that people could literally access millions of book titles without ever leaving their homes was a key factor in the Amazon "completed" product.

In other situations, place might be a negotiated marketing agreement that inserts a message for your product in a partner's marketing materials. If you can be creative and negotiate partner marketing deals that get you access to your customers at lower prices than your competitors, that is a strong competitive advantage. The point we're making here is that when you think about your completed product, be sure to be as creative as possible in thinking about how place can help shape that product.

Packaging

To appreciate fully how powerful the role packaging can play in completing or becoming your product, you only have to look at the little blue boxes in which all Tiffany jewelry products are packaged. Whether it's a watch or a bracelet or a ring, somehow that gift is seen as more valuable when it arrives in a Tiffany box or velveteen bag. There is no need to look at the actual product—the assumption before the gift is even opened is that it is of absolute quality, and that you took time and care in making the purchase. One could make the argument that what Tiffany really sells is not quality jewelry, but the perception that the jewelry is of the highest quality, and that perception somehow has been translated into the Tiffany package.

Promotion

You may not know of Gevalia Coffees, but they are a very fine maker of a wide variety of coffees. The coffee is very good, but their genius is not in the fine coffee they deliver through direct marketing, but the way they incorporate promotion into their product offering. Every time you buy something from Gevalia, they reward you with a gift that links you back into a purchase. For example, if you just buy six more packages of selected coffees, you will get a beautiful and exclusive Gevalia coffeemaker. While you may feel you have more than enough coffee for now, the lure of that beautiful coffeemaker is almost irresistible, and all of a sudden more Gevalia coffee appears on your doorstep.

Another example of a company using promotion as a key in its product offering is the newest of the direct marketers of flowers. While 1-800-Flowers.com pioneered the market for direct selling of flowers, they mainly used television advertising and phone. ProFlowers, on the other hand, is a master of using the Internet and ongoing e-mail promotions to build sales to new and existing customers. ProFlowers uses event promotions heavily to attract new customers. For example, at Valentine's Day they deliver extraordinary offers on roses. Once you purchase from them they include you in their Customer Relationship Management (CRM) database, and from then on their competitive advantage is that they can promote new offers to you at little or no expense. ProFlowers's core product is a commodity—flowers are flowers, after all, and they can be purchased anywhere from your supermarket to flower shop. But ProFlowers's completed product includes the brilliance and frequency with which they promote in specific ways to their existing customers. ProFlowers's core product might be flowers, but their completed product might be better defined as one of the world's best promotional databases. Their example is one we can all follow.

Augmented Product

If there is one way to truly add value to your product it is through augmentation or enhancement strategies. This is where the market research you've done in talking and listening to your customers to find out what their deep-down issues or concerns are can really pay off in entrepreneurial success. The best way to understand this in a nontheoretical way is by looking at some examples.

We're Not Selling Makeup, We're Selling Hope

It may be an oversimplification to say that all sales are emotional, but it is a rule of thumb that won't steer you wrong. On a flight several years ago, Michael met a business school friend who was now a senior financial officer for one of the world's largest cosmetic companies. He had previously been a financial officer for a heavy equipment manufacturer, where cost of the product was a key component in being competitive in the marketplace. After working in the cosmetic industry for several years, he was still amazed by the fact that there was absolutely no correlation between the cost of producing their product and the price for which it was sold. As our friend said, "When we make a perfume, the most expensive part of this product is the bottle we put it in." This is a great reminder that what your customer is purchasing may rarely be what your core product is. As the founder of Revlon, Charles Revson supposedly said, when confronted by someone who asked how he could charge so much for a perfume that cost so little to produce, "We're not selling cosmetics, we're selling hope." On a rational level, there is no way that women should spend $50–$500 for a bottle of fragrance that may only cost pennies to manufacture. But when you understand what they are really buying—the assurance that they will be perceived as more attractive and that this little bottle is the key to something they can't get anywhere else—you understand why Revson became a business legend.

Roadside Assistance, Not Cars

Another example that shows exactly how understanding what your customers really want can help you shape your product in uniquely effective ways is some work Michael did with a major car brand several years ago. In this case, he was helping a client build a sales and referral program for a specific target audience that had been largely ignored by the auto industry—divorced and widowed women over sixty. These women were ideal potential customers. They had money and they had the desire to purchase cars because being independent was key to their self-image, but there was one major barrier to their involvement with any car brand: no car brand seemed to want these buyers. When they walked into a dealership, they were often ignored or asked where their husband was. In addition, there was an additional hidden emotional issue that created a barrier to purchase. Most simply, if they were on the road and the car broke down, who would come get them? This is an emotional issue for all of us, but specifically for older women who were divorced or whose husbands had passed away. Much more important than car price, looks, or features was this simple and paramount emotional issue. In our marketing to this previously ignored market group, we highlighted a product benefit—24/7 roadside assistance that answered this question and changed the true nature of the augmented product from a car to special service.

To create a uniquely augmented product, you don't have to be an inventor of new benefits. It is all about what you focus on and communicate to your customers. As you think about what your customers truly want, remember that you can augment the product in almost endless ways

Differentiated Product

When selling any product, it is always powerful to be able to show how your product is different—the unique benefits that would prompt a customer to buy your products rather than your competitors'. Many entrepreneurs we work with focus on creating differences that are different in degree. Their product is an "er" product: faster, cheaper, better, tastier, bigger, smaller, etc. That they have a clear differentiator is good, but differences in degree are often difficult to demonstrate, communicate, or prove. A claim that your pizza is tastier, for example, is subjective and hard to substantiate.

"Only": The Very Best Way to Differentiate Your Product

While it is certainly good to have degree differences, it is even better if you can find a way to differentiate your product in an absolute way, what we call a "difference in kind." And the clearest way to do that is to find a product feature that is absolutely unique. When you are the company that has the only widget in the world, assuming that the world needs and wants widgets, you have a very strong enhanced product position.

Protecting Your Product's Intellectual Value

In the days of the Gold Rush, we thought of owning property as the key to wealth. Would-be miners flooded California with the dream of striking it rich by finding the right piece of property that had gold on it. That property was protected through deeds and titles.

As we move into a business world in which intellectual property, the product of our minds, becomes recognized as a new source of wealth, we need new ways to protect our property. Intellectual property law has evolved rapidly to address the needs of the new type of entrepreneurs. Depending on the nature of your business, you will want to get as much legal protection for your business concept or products as possible. The most complete protection is a patent; it is also the most expensive and difficult to acquire. The easiest to get is a Confidentiality Agreement (also known as a Non-Disclosure Agreement or NDA.) We recommend protecting everything you invent or develop in every way you can—use trademarks, copyrights, patents, and confidentiality agreements in a complete way. For some of the more complex protections you will want to consult an attorney, but here's a quick primer on some of the more basic forms of protection.

Confidentiality Agreements

This is one of the most basic legal documents you must have as you start to discuss your business concept with potential investors, management members, and strategic partners. Often, these contain standardized language but make sure that your agreements are tailored to the nature of your business and really address the issues about which you are most concerned. If your business or invention is technical in nature, you need to be especially careful with the protection you can get through this kind of agreement.

Copyrights

The next basic protection is to make sure you copyright everything you write—this certainly needs to include all of the business presentations, PowerPoints, executive summaries, and other materials you produce, even if they are never going to be formally published. Inserting the words "Confidential" and "Copyright" (and appropriate year) by your corporate entity is a must do. And of course, all of the marketing materials, brochures, commercials, advertisements, and website materials you create or are created for you need to be copyrighted as well. Copyright is a much more technical issue than described here, especially if you are in a business that involves formal publishing, whether of software, print, film, video, or internet media. You need to pay special attention to copyright protection and seek the advice of specialist attorneys in this field. Copyright is a basic protection of your intellectual property—what you write or communicate—and you should use it everywhere.

Trademarks

As you develop marketing materials for your firm, division, or products you will want to create a trademarked look and feel for those materials. When you think about whether trademarking something is important or not, think of McDonald's. They own many trademarks, and many of those trademarks are among the most valuable and protected assets of the firm. Golden Arches and Big Mac are not just concepts, they are intellectual property, and they have produced billions of dollars of profit for their owners.

Trademark law requires specialist attorneys, and if trademarks are going to be a key to your business (typically, they are very valuable in consumer-driven marketing businesses), you will want to start, at the minimum, putting "TM" after every use of a trademark you have created. Consult an attorney on the processes necessary for protecting your key trademarks.

Technical Patents

According to Bill Walker, an attorney who works exclusively with start-up firms, the gaining and maintenance of patents is a highly specialized area of law, and even experienced legal practitioners need to consult absolute patent specialists, like Wendy Buskop, the founder and lead partner in Buskop Law. If your product or business concept is a technical one, software, hardware, Internet, scientific, or mechanical, you need especially to consult with a strong patent lawyer. As Walker points out, many patent attorneys are more comfortable working with very large corporations. Timeframes are longer and expenses are larger with these firms. They do a great job, but they do it for larger firms. But don't despair, because there are firms like Buskop Law, that are well-versed in large-firm patent work, are entrepreneurial in spirit, and make a living working with start-up firms. A patent application and effort that might take months with a larger firm can often be done in half the time or less when using a firm that understands the needs of entrepreneurs. According to Buskop, "The patent office has actually changed, in a positive way. Many of the examiners for patents are actually looking for ways to help you get your patent. If approached in a nonadversarial way, they can help direct the patent applicant to perfect his application in a way that will allow him to gain the protection he or she is seeking."

Depending on your funding and the importance of patent protection, you may seek out larger patent attorneys—they, by definition, are all highly skilled and specialized experts. We suggest that patent protection may be available even for relatively small start-ups if you find the right attorneys. How much money are we discussing? Let's say it may be done for less than $10,000. If you want a patent for the power of raising money, that is a relatively small investment. If you are looking for the ultimate protection of your entire business, it is an absolute necessity.

Business Process Patents

A new opportunity for intellectual property protection is a relatively new development that opens up patent protection to nontechnical inventions. Many people think that to apply or gain a patent you have to be someone like Thomas Edison. In this new world of patent protection you don't need a laboratory, you don't need to be a scientist, you don't need to be an inventor, and you don't need to live in Silicon Valley. Amazingly, what you need to do is develop a new business model or process. Many people don't even know that this kind of work can be patented. But again, according to Buskop, many firms want business process patents to protect their start-up ideas.

Intellectual Property 101

We've stressed the importance of ensuring your products and your processes against both fair and unfair competition to foster both the survival and the growth of your enterprise. We've emphasized the importance of innovation to your business's success. If you've taken us seriously and followed our advice, above all, you need to know how to protect your intellectual property. Whether your proprietary material involves an invention, a process, a design or the creative expression of ideas and concepts, these are tangible assets that add value to your business. These assets may ultimately impact the price you can command for your products and services as well as the price you may sell your business for in the future.

So, what do the experts say about how to protect your property? Robert Kovelman, Esq., of the California law firm Steptoe & Johnson (*www.steptoe.com*), advises that under current law, you don't want to talk to anyone about your invention before you protect it. Don't sell yourself short. While articles tell you to talk to your friends—don't. In today's world of viral marketing, you risk having your work proliferate, become public, and losing any chance of protection. Kovelman advises you to think outside the box. He says, "See if an invention will work outside the specific industry you designed it for, if it might have a broader reach. Anything manufactured under the sun by man is protectable. You can even protect your business methods as a process."

Let's define the various categories of protection, so you can see what applies to your business:

A utility patent protects structure and function. An apparatus (device) belongs to a system (a device used in combination with other components) or to a method (the steps you take to accomplish something).

A design patent protects the ornamental appearance of something.

So, how does Kovelman recommend you undertake the process of protection? Apply for protection through the government; document the times and dates you invented the item, and above all, keep good records of what you've done. Seek help to prepare the application. We live and work in a global village; keep in mind that a U.S. patent only protects you in the United States. You must apply for foreign protection country by country.

So, where do you find qualified, competent help? Kovelman advises going to the U.S. Patent Office's official website, *www. uspto.gov*, and finding a list of registered patent attorneys. In addition, seek out referrals through other inventors or through venture capital associations, etc.

What other types of protection exist? The patent may not always provide the best protection. If you want to exclude others from making an item with a specific structure and function, seek patent protection. On the other hand, the recipe for Coca-Cola is a trade secret; it has an indefinite shelf life. It is not known to the public. This provides you with an economic advantage. You need to evaluate timing issues; in the case of technology, such as software, where getting to market quickly becomes paramount, you may be better off not filing for patent protection. Instead, Kovelman recommends, publish it on a website so others won't use it.

Let's look at other types of protection that may apply to your proprietary creations. Trademarks identify the source of a product or a service while copyrights protect the expression of an idea. Notice that we did not say "protect an idea." An idea alone does not qualify for protection. Trade secrets, on the other hand, protect something not generally known by the public and provide you with some economic advantage. They also can't be reverse engineered. That's when a would-be competitor analyzes the makeup, structure, or formulation of your product and attempts to duplicate it. We mentioned the example of the formula for Coca-Cola. Locked in a safe and known to only a select few, it has longer protection than a statutory patent.

What about licensing? This method of protection involves a way of getting a return on your investment, either offensively or defensively. Use a license to get into markets you couldn't normally get into. License a technology to avoid someone suing you. You can make the license exclusive or it can give someone the right to practice what is in the patent. You can make it nonexclusive, with limited use for a restricted geography, time period, or a specific type of product or application. For example, in a landmark case known as the Metamune Case, the licensee challenged the validity of the patent. Keep in mind that patent litigation is among the most expensive—starting at a minimum cost of about $2 million, according to Kovelman.

After documenting all of your steps in creating your intellectual property and seeking out qualified counsel, avoid any placement of your invention or process into public usage, sale, or knowledge until you have actually applied for patent protection. One recent change in the landscape involves what we refer to as "patent trolls." These investors own intellectual property and patents. They can assert their ownership for the purpose of filing infringement suits. At this writing, legislation is pending in Congress. If passed, the Patent Reform Act would alter rights and damages, limiting the damages these patent trolls can collect.

Are the intellectual property laws themselves ensured? According to Kovelman, no. "Laws become difficult to apply, due to the rapid changes in today's technological world. Take for example, the Digital Millenium Copyright Act (the law designed to protect intellectual property in the era of the World Wide Web). Technology has outpaced the law. Congress will need to pass expansive overhauls and changes. If people are not incentivized to create, they will not."

Once again, before you release your creations on the world, think globally when it comes to protecting them. Rules vary by country. China has been notorious for not respecting intellectual property, but they are starting to enforce it more, since they are becoming a world player. The conundrum is that start-ups frequently don't have the money to protect intellectual property, yet if they don't protect it, they can lose it. Kovelman's advice is to file a provisional patent application, which gives you a year to see if it's a good idea. It's a place-holder; after a year, you lose the priority to receive protection if you don't file a formal patent application. Keep in mind that intellectual property is dynamic, living, and breathing. If the invention is core to what your company is going to be doing, it should be protected.

Before you start, talk to a qualified counselor and find out your options. As always, *caveat emptor*—buyer beware, as we say. Some of the companies advertising their services in mass media may secure a design patent without getting you structure and function coverage. They may disclose confidential information to the marketplace in the process. The protections you lose could cost you far more in the long run. It's simply not the same as hiring a qualified patent attorney. Drug companies use patents to keep others out of the market, due to their large expenditures for research and development. Film studios have similarly bought copyrights to scripts for movies they never intended to produce, simply to prevent rival studios from releasing them.

On a real nuts and bolts level, Kovelman advises keeping good records that document when you invented the item. Have someone who is not an interested party sign them. Any external source that corroborates what you say is beneficial. If someone filed for protection before you, but you can prove that you invented the item first, you can revoke her patent (commonly known as an interference). You need to weigh the cost benefit of protection; is it useful outside of your area of interest? For how long? Will it provide you a defensive posture (commonly known as trade bait)? A bargaining chip? Does it make your product better or make it function better? It's a return-on-investment (ROI) issue.

Kovelman advises, "People come in with really good ideas; marketing them for two years; then try to seek a patent. They can't do it. Find out your options sooner."

Smart-Start Summary: *Sure-Fire Ways to Create a Successful Product Line*

1. Consider ways to enhance and augment your product offerings.
2. Price, Place, and Promotion can be key ways to augment your products.
3. "Only" can be the strongest way to differentiate your product; look for ways you can be different in kind, not just in degree.
4. Use all possible means to protect your intellectual property.
5. Weigh the cost benefits of protecting your property in a competitive world.

Chapter

6

Generate Smart-Start Marketing

By marketing we mean the sum total of all your efforts to bring your product or service from the producer to the ultimate consumer. By definition, marketing involves the process by which we move goods and services from producer to end user. It involves the proper sequence of carefully planned steps designed to identify who your prospects are, how to best deliver them, how to best communicate with them, what they like and dislike most about your competitors' products, and what it would take to get them to switch to your products or services. The marketing umbrella covers everything from researching consumer behavior to studying the competitive landscape to planning a successful media strategy to creating messages that will resonate with your customers to penetrating the ideal distribution channels to developing and executing strategies to retain customers.

Smart-Start Marketing encompasses the following:

- **Market research:** The study of the universe of your potential consumers, who they are, what they buy, how they buy, when and where they buy, where they live, and what drives their decisions.
- **Advertising:** The art and science of telling your company and/or product story to your potential consumers, including the selection of the most efficient and effective media, as well as devising and executing the most motivating message.
- **Promotion:** The showcasing of special opportunities to trigger a consumer purchase.
- **Publicity:** The process of engaging the media to tell the newsworthy aspects of your story.
- **Customer relationship management:** The continuing engagement with the consumer following the sale to maintain a level of satisfaction.

♦ **Merchandising:** The process of creating the most enticing product displays, offers and packaging.

Customer relationships are your most important asset; yet many companies focus on customer acquisition and ignore on-going customer development. Don't make the same mistake. Viewed in the above context, the goals of marketing are to gain and maintain customers, foster repeat purchases, and encourage referrals. What happens after the first sale, can be the key to your ultimate business success.

To Research or Not to Research

Always know that arrogance will be your undoing. Assume you know nothing when you first undertake marketing any product or service. If you must make any assumptions at all, test them. Years ago Barry was working with a start-up in the home-based learning field. He stressed the need for and the importance of conducting market research. While they had tested the viability of their product and carefully researched their competition's price points, they outright refused to do further research on their delivery system. Instead, they insisted that only the advertising needed testing.

In a very short time, they had burned through their investors' money and had not generated enough response to cover the costs of producing and shipping the product or for additional advertising. The reality was they had produced a product consisting of a box full of books and tapes that might have sold well twenty years earlier. At the time of their launch, the entire system could have been delivered on a single CD-ROM. This would have cost less in the long run to produce, less to warehouse and ship, and would have had far more appeal to the current generation of computer-literate young adults and their children.

SMART-START TIP

Every dollar spent on market research is an investment that pays
off in much greater cost savings and sales down the road.

!

When you launch a new product, even after you become
a well-established company, treat the new product launch the
same as you would a start-up. Even the biggest, brightest, and
best have failed to do this—with disastrous results. Coca-Cola,
the undisputed leader in the soft drink industry, failed miserably
when they launched their line extensions several years ago. With
New Coke, Old Coke, Diet Coke, etc., they confused consumers
and ended up diluting their market share.

Diamond Crystal Salt decided to change its packaging several years ago. A small problem resulted—many of their best
customers, heavy users of salt, were Hispanics. The new package
did not tell these loyal consumers in their native language—or
the general population—that it was the same product, simply
repackaged. Once again, a small investment in market research
might have revealed this critical detail and avoided the loss of
sales from people who did not recognize their favorite brand
and therefore did not purchase it.

Protect Your Advertising Investment with Your Research

As a start-up you can't afford to make costly mistakes. The more
intelligence you gather the more you increase your chances for
success. How do you put this knowledge to work for your fledgling company? In today's world, you cannot sell to everyone; we
live in a fragmented world. Groups of people travel in different
circles, practice different lifestyles, have different travel patterns,

associate with different people. They read, watch, and listen to different media and purchase through entirely different distribution channels.

First and foremost, use your market research to determine exactly who will buy your product or service. As a start-up you don't have unlimited funds. Look for the quickest return on investment. Find the heavy-user groups for your product or service. Identify both their lifestyles and their life stages. Are they young, urban, ethnic minorities concentrated in the cities with the ten largest populations? Are they Asian Americans with advanced degrees, employed in high-tech industries? Are they affluent, aging baby boomers at the peak of their careers, with high net worth?

Once you identify the best prospects for your product or service, learn everything you can about their current purchasing power, habits, and preferences. Do they earn well yet spend at or above their means? How price sensitive are they? Do they prefer big box discount stores, malls and department stores, catalogs or Internet purchasing? What competitive products or services do they buy now? What do they like most about them? What do they like least about them? Most importantly, what would it take to make them switch to your product or service? Guess how you find out. You got it! Ask, and keep asking them. Nobody can and will tell you more of what you need to know than your own potential customers.

Now, put the intelligence to work. List your competitive advantages. If possible, create new ones to fill the gaps left by your competitors. Those advantages can include:

- Actual (intrinsic) product or service attributes
- Greater convenience, availability, or improved delivery
- More credible endorsements, awards, or positive publicity
- Better value proposition
- Stronger warranty or better after-sale service
- Repeat purchase incentives

Let's examine these. The most important elements you glean from your research become your central advertising message—your key copy points. For example, we conducted focus groups for an operator of six cemetery properties. We learned that affluent suburbanites aged forty-five to sixty-four considering pre-purchasing burial plots wanted assurances that the properties had nice locations, were well maintained, and were operated by a credible, responsible company that would be around when they needed them twenty or thirty years from now. The free and heavily discounted offers the company promoted simply did not resonate with them. Moreover, today's consumer did not want a salesperson making a house call. Instead, they wanted to review information privately and respond if they had an interest. This changed the entire ad copy approach to one that outlined the consumer's choices and changed the call to action, driving respondents to a dedicated webpage.

So, now that you know who wants to buy your product how do you craft your message to appeal to them? Remember, you can't sell auto parts the same way you sell cosmetics. Consider the look (or sound) and feel of the ad, the tone and the execution or presentation of the ad. It will resonate with your target audience only if you produce the right materials. Return to your research. Asking consumers to respond to different potential advertising approaches and offers can help you ferret out the right direction for your advertising. Remember at all times that very few purchases are totally intellectual. Make sure you appeal to your buyers' emotions. Even business-to-business advertising needs some degree of emotional appeal. Consider this example, you sell office equipment. The purchasing manager doesn't care, but the administrative assistant who will use it and her boss the sales manager that depends on her work do care about the stress-free service plan that comes with it.

So, what if you identified the right people to talk to, produced the right message, but you don't know where to find them? Enter the media professionals. Fortunately for you, most of today's major advertising media have sophisticated enough research to tell you precisely who reads, watches, or listens to them. Don't get taken in by statements like, "They're paying for cable television, so they must be watching it" or, "Everyone in town reads our paper/listens to our station." Demand the proof.

Welcome to the match game. Check your customer research against their research and see if you can find a match. Ultimately, the formula for success dictates that the media deliver the greatest number of qualified purchasers for the least cost. Notice we said qualified. Avoid the temptation to just buy quantity—sheer numbers of readers, viewers, or listeners could result in paying to reach a high percentage of unqualified prospects, or as we say, suspects.

Hire Mercenaries to Take the Bullets

You may be thinking you don't have time for this, that if you met with every ad salesperson from every media outlet you would never launch and run your business. Our advice to you: Don't try this at home. Hire independent advertising counsel. Good advertising counsel will make you money (by getting better results) and save you money (with greater negotiating clout), not cost you money. Here's why. A well-established advertising agency with a knowledgeable staff buys more space and time in the media, more Internet advertising, more printing, more recording, more videography for its stable of clients than you will buy for your start-up. This gives them more weight to throw around, resulting in better pricing. In addition, most major media already include the agency's commission for placing the time or space, so it doesn't cost you more for them to place it. It may cost you less because of the volume of business they place with the media. More importantly, the agency's knowledge should result in better-targeted media buys, which will mean a better return on investment for you. Equally important, a better designed and executed creative campaign will bring better results—which can pay for itself many times over.

Suppose you sell a high-quality product. You need a high-quality company perception. Quality sells quality. If your ad campaign screams bargain basement even if you're exposing it to an audience with the buying power, they will not respond to the campaign if they don't believe you can deliver on the product's promises. Remember, perception is reality.

Your advertising is the face of your product that you show to the world. More today than ever before, we live in a world where people demand instant gratification People judge your business in seconds. If your website takes too long to load, is difficult to navigate, or looks amateurish, you may have lost a sale and a prospective customer, with all of her repeat purchases and referrals. In short, make sure your first impression to a customer is the right one. For a more complete discussion of how to select and work with advertising counsel, see our other book, *10 Ways to Screw Up an Ad Campaign.*

A Brand by any Other Name Might Not Smell as Sweet

First of all, let's be clear about what a brand is and isn't. Recently, Barry sat on a panel about marketing. When the graphic designer on his left began to abuse the "B" word (branding), he could not help myself. He piped up, "Dave, let's be careful not to confuse a brand with brand indicia. Campbell's soup is not red and white, it's the expectation of consistent delivery of a set of attributes—like the warm feeling you get when you crack open the Campbell's Soup. When Ted over there gets into his Saab, he doesn't expect it to drive like a Yugo."

Brand equity is even more complex. In Michael's work with large companies, he challenged them to look at brand equity as gender and cultural life stage-appropriate benefits that guaranteed repeat purchase of the product at a fair price. This is far different than brand awareness, which many people confuse with the power of a brand. While Coke may be the best-known brand on the planet, having an extremely high level of brand awareness, its brand equity may be slipping if it has to discount its prices aggressively each weekend or be outsold by Pepsi.

Fran Lytle of Brand Champs, a consultancy that has worked with many large companies, has this to add: "Brands are living, breathing entities, like people. Understanding that helps your customers enter into a relationship with your brand. That means they can be forgiving, as well. For example, when Tylenol experienced the tampering scandal, they had already done such a good job of earning people's trust that customers were willing to maintain their relationship with the brand. The value of a brand is not only in its product efficacy or its functional aspects, because that can be parroted. Rather, the value is in the brand's ability to create emotional bonds with people and help people to understand how their lives will be positively impacted by entering into a relationship with that brand."

Michael, who actually consulted for and created strategies for Tylenol, also likes Tylenol as an example of the power of brand equity. He notes that, "Tylenol is perhaps one of the clearest and most direct examples of the economic impact of brand power, since it is priced almost twice as much as generic acetaminophen—which is, by law, exactly what Tylenol is." In other words, the brand "Tylenol" contributes double the value of the brand acetaminophen, and they are exactly the same physical product. What explains this kind of economic value addition that appears to be irrational? In Tylenol's case, as Michael points out, it is the trust that customers give to the brand. There is an emotional connection that makes it worth the extra money.

As an entrepreneur looking at building your own company's brand, remember that emotional connection is hugely important. Is a meal at the famous Charlie Trotter's restaurant all that much better than one at hundreds of many other good restaurants that charge far less? Is Screaming Eagle Cabernet, worth $500 per bottle while other fine California cabernets are being sold for $25? They are indeed, at least to some consumers who value the emotional extra that these brands deliver. It's a lesson that any entrepreneur should value: Marketing your products is as much about capturing a share of your customers' hearts as it is about presenting a purely rational benefit picture that may or may not motivate them to buy.

As an entrepreneur, a developer of new products, how can you differentiate your brand? Lytle advises, "Look at it from the customer's need state, not from the new product aspect." For example, the Lytles worked with the CEO of Coakley Business Class. The owner sought to develop a better way for business-women to travel—a one-bag solution. She had experienced the frustration over the limitations of carry-on luggage and airline restrictions on how many bags a woman could carry. The result: a patented organizational solution. However, in order to sell more product she needed to understand that she could also address the needs of female urban commuters and suburban moms. In short, she had to allow herself to see all women in all need states, lifestyles, and life stages.

As a smart-start entrepreneur when you look at your marketing, make sure that it is also life-stage relevant. Even many sophisticated marketers ignore this key concept, which is increasingly important as we develop a broad and multigenerational buying audience. As a consultant, Michael helped companies like Kemper and General Motors better understand that their brands had a generic message, even though the products were designed to meet the needs of multiple audiences, and this could be highly counter-productive. He points out that the same brand attributes that may appeal to one group or life-stage segment can frighten off or repel others. A good example of this is some brand work Michael did for Wells Fargo. In this bank's direct marketing they were featuring fast growth in the stocks they were recommending to their bank customers. While this benefit may well appeal to a younger life stage willing to take risks, that same claim focused on an issue that scared their older, retired life-stage customers who wanted security in their investments above all else.

Additionally, when thinking about brand positioning and benefits, be aware of gender, racial, ethnic, and cultural issues. For example, when marketing to widowed or divorced women over sixty-five on behalf of Buick, Michael created very successful programs based on the absolutely key issues that separated what these women most valued from a car company. And those issues were far different from the issues that had motivated their husbands to purchase and identify with their car brands. For example, the key issues for these older, widowed women were not how the car looked, how fast it drove, or what it cost. Their key issues were who would come and get them if the car broke down and how comfortable they would be with the car salesman. In the marketing campaigns that Michael and his team created, the focus was on those two issues—that Buick provided road-side assistance and would come get them and that their salesmen were specially trained to deal sensitively with single, older women. Not only did the program generate sales from the women who received these direct-mail pieces, they also generated sales from their friends—referrals that these women created. You can learn more about these approaches at the website: *www.LifeStageMarketing.com*.

Author's note: Fran and Bill Lytle conduct workshops on branding and their e-mail and print materials can be useful to entrepreneurs with businesses of any size. Visit them at *www.BrandChamps.com*.

We asked Fran what the single most important step a start-up business can and should take to enhance and protect its products would be. The answer: "They have to do some real soul searching. The product has to address a need state to succeed. Entrepreneurs get excited; they forget to ask other people if their product is for them, for someone else, for whom?" Fran urges do it formally or informally, but do it.

Get a Leg Up on Your Competitors with Promotions

To kick response levels up without increasing your advertising budget you may want to engage in promotion. Promotion can take several forms. The most common involves selling off–price. How you present the opportunity makes all the difference in your response rate. Make the savings as tangible as you can. Make them appear as attractive as you can. As a general rule, give real dollar savings people can relate to. They nearly always pull better results than percentages.

Don't ignore special-event promotions, especially if you sell at retail locations. When people see a crowd, they gather around. When possible, conduct live demonstrations. You can sell a lot more knives when someone prepares food with them than you can on a display rack. Event-oriented promotions give you a chance to get close to your customer, create a memorable experience, and entice them back.

Tie in to major holidays, celebrations, sporting events, festivals, concerts, etc., to coat-tail existing excitement that already attracts a similar customer profile. Engage in promoting your support of cause-related marketing. If you support your customers' favorite charities, they will, in turn, support you—but only if they know you are behind them.

Promotion gives your advertising extra fire power, just don't abuse it—it will kill your credibility and your pricing structure. Watch your regulatory agencies here. Some states require you to disclose manufacturers' suggested prices, everyday (regular) prices, the amount of savings, and how long the sale price will be honored.

Publicity: How the Internet Lets You Teach "Cats to Bark"

One dramatic example of how the Internet has changed traditional marketing is in the ease with which you can generate publicity. In the past, you would have to hire a public relations firm and let them work their contacts to specific media. Major media controlled stories, and you were largely at their mercy. With Internet sites like PR.com or PRWeb, and access to the wild world of blogs, that has dramatically changed. In the past, PR was seldom free. The average business would pay a public relations firm a retainer of several thousand dollars a month to get that "free" press. We're not saying that PR professionals shouldn't be used. Depending on your budget, and the size and scope of your business, they may be able to accelerate your PR efforts dramatically. However, unlike the past, you now have alternatives. For example, when launching their book *Waiting for Your Cat to Bark*, a great book on the art of persuading customers to do what you would like, Jeffrey and Bryan Eisenberg sent out Internet Press Releases everyday well in advance of the book's publication. Bloggers interested in the points they were making starting writing their own articles about the book. Other bloggers started responding, and by the time the book was actually published, there was a strong developed market for it. In addition, the web publicity and " buzz" about their book, drove potential customers to their website, where they offer consulting services on web marketing.

In this case, resulting in a perfect closed circle of marketing success. In the past, PR and advertising performed very different roles. Public relations (PR) created a climate favorable to sales; advertising drove traffic and sales. Public relations gave you credibility in the marketplace so your advertising rang true. The PR effort is what others say about you; your advertising is what you say about yourself. Practitioners often say, "You pay for advertising; you pray for PR." You can't control the timing, the message, or the placement with PR, but you can with advertising. This in some ways is still true—however, the Internet and your ability to access PR directly is changing this world, and blurring the lines between advertising and PR, all in a way that benefits a smaller, smart-start company.

Without question, positive press can enhance the success of a start-up. In most cases, however, it doesn't happen overnight. Even the best publicists need time to plant a story. Overworked, short-staffed editors and producers become inundated with requests. It can take weeks or even months before they get to your story. But—and this is a major "but"—the Internet allows you to change your PR story often until you find something that bloggers or editors feel compelled to publish. Being persistent is key. Most importantly, however, your story has to be newsworthy.

For example, we are working with a woman who has a device for pregnancy and fertility testing. That's not the full, PR-able story. In her case, the human-interest story has power. She emigrated to the United States as a single mother with only $800 in her pocket, bought a house in two years, succeeded in a job, then left her job to promote a product she discovered that could help others avoid her own near-death health crisis. Do you see the difference? And of course, however you gain positive PR, whether it's on the Internet, or in traditional media, you will want to constantly feature it in your advertising and merchandising.

Merchandising

Just as the presentation of your ad campaign positions your product in consumers' minds as something they will or will not gravitate to, the physical merchandising of your product will either attract or repel your target customer. Make sure you understand what resonates with them. Make sure the presentation is congruent with the level of product you sell. A Rolls-Royce buyer expects the showroom to look rich; a Kia buyer does not.

Home Depot advertises their brand as a cost-conscious choice. Their stores properly have a warehouse look. If you invest your life's savings with a boutique financial planning firm, you expect the offices to look professional and to speak wealth. Even the staff's clothing should make the same statement. Apparel retailers understood this distinction early in the game. They have always made the choice to display their merchandise with a showroom that reflected their value perception—either plush or pipe racks. The value-conscious consumer believes they are paying for the high overhead in pricier department stores. Instead, they gravitate to the mass merchandiser that conveys a more no-frills environment.

As an entrepreneur of any size business, the idea that your merchandising is congruent with your value proposition is keenly important. If you are opening an upscale French restaurant, the menus, tablecloths, and silverware all have to bespeak that level of quality. If you are opening a value-oriented dry cleaner, perhaps the major merchandising message only needs to be big signs on your windows that claim "All shirts cleaned for 99 cents." The key is to match your merchandising with your message.

How to Succeed with Your Customer Relationship Management

Remember, we want your start-up to succeed every step of the way. Retaining a customer is just as important as attracting one. In fact, we would claim, and there is a lot of evidence to support this, retaining customers and getting them to refer your business is the key indicator of whether your business will succeed over the long term. Many leading businesses have been using something called NPS (or Net Promoter Score) to see how well they are actually doing with their customers, and we strongly recommend you take this innovative concept to heart. Developed by one of the pioneers in customer loyalty, Fred Reichheld, a Bain consultant, the NPS is calculated by surveying your customers to find out how many would positively refer your firm, those who are neutral, and those who are negative. Reichheld shows very convincingly that companies with positive NPSs are great performers. To learn more about this, see his book *The Ultimate Question* or go to the website, *www.TheUltimateQuestion.com.*

To improve your ability to manage your customers' long-term loyalties, make sure you have a system in place to capture data, track who is buying from you, what they buy, how much, how often, and what they spend. Marketing to your existing customers can cost you far less than acquiring new customers. Showing customers you care and you value their patronage pays big dividends in the form of loyalty, which translates into more repeat sales, more incremental sales, and more referrals.

Customer relationship management (CRM) is no accident. It's a carefully planned program. In our computer age, it's easier, less time consuming, and more accurate to conduct a CRM program than ever before. And perhaps most importantly, the Internet has removed the major barrier to on-going customer relationships, cost. In the past, it was just very expensive to stay in touch with your customers. E-mail has changed all that. By acquiring your customers email addresses as a routine part of your business practice, you are building what many entrepreneurs now regard as their most important asset—a database of your customers. There are now many off-the-shelf customer database programs available, and many of them are very inexpensive; yet they can give a small business real tools to manage customers. For example, you can cull through and find the customers that spent the highest dollar amount and those that made the greatest number of purchases from you. Now, examine what products or services they bought and which ones they did not buy. Then, send them a mailing, an e-mailing, or call them to cross-sell them the products they did not buy. Even a start-up can engage in CRM. In fact, the earlier you do, the greater the customer loyalty and the more incremental sales and referrals you will create. As your product line grows, you will continue to expand your revenue base from your existing customers, while acquiring new customers. Include a referral program as an incentive to your current customers so they send friends and families to you as potential customers. Give them discounts or other bonuses for doing so. Think about this: Every customer who refers another customer has just reduced your marketing expense by half.

TOM MESSNER: Real-World Marketing Success

Tom Messner, is a founding partner of the ad agency Messner, Vettere, Schmetterer, and Bergere, which he eventually sold to Eurocom (*www.eurorscg.com*), one of the two worldwide advertising agency syndicates. He worked on many of the most prestigious brands that comprise today's landscape. We asked him to look back at his own days as a start-up as well as his clients' early marketing efforts.

Q: When you and your partners started your business, what unique ways did you market yourselves?

A: We got a lot of attention doing a governor's race; the advertising got high-profile PR. We did self-promo PR. For example, when (former Russian Premier) Gorbachev visited New York, we ran a *New York Times* ad inviting him to see our business. We had done an ad for (former U.S. President) George H.W. Bush. Channel 5 in New York interviewed us. We hired a well-known publicist—he got us in *Fortune* magazine. We sought to make ourselves look much bigger than we were. Very few agencies do this. Chiat-Day and Young & Rubicam did so. Jordan-Case-McGrath placed commercials for their clients in a movie, book-ending it with ads for themselves. Chiat-Day ran an ad when they lost Apple, thanking them (for the privilege of serving them).

Q: What marketing mistakes did you make in your own business, and how did you correct them?

A: Selling the agency versus buying it back; we thought our chances for growth were limited without an international presence. Some of the larger clients required an overseas presence.

Q: What smart marketing moves did your clients make early in the game?

A: In our second year, Nasdaq had no identity. They were viewed as risky investments. We positioned them as a Stock Exchange and we portrayed it as a new way to trade stocks and raise money. We showed that companies like Microsoft, Intel, and MCI were at the forefront of transforming American business. We were close to the CEO of MCI. MCI was being destroyed by AT&T's advertising. They hired us in part because of our political experience. Volvo had a bad experience with a previous agency; they had been embarrassed by a falsified commercial. Bob Schmetterer had worked on Volvo and at Volvo; he had a great connection philosophically. They liked the agency's ability to handle crisis. Plus, we were resilient.

Q: What are the most important marketing tips you can offer to start-ups?

A: Mary Wells of Wells, Rich & Greene advised, "Do it; if you don't, you will always wonder." Use media to make yourself look bigger than you are—get early credibility— it saves us a lot of time. You have to have a lot of things going for you first. We had four partners and vest-pocket accounts; we got leads from people that moved on to other companies.

Q: What was at the core of your business' growth strategy?

A: See the article "Birth of an Agency" in *Adweek* magazine. We did a miniature golf tournament. I was an Adweek columnist for three years. Fallon-McElligott used awards as a marketing tool. We had a tech advantage over our competitors—we were communicating electronically earlier than the rest were.

Q: What would you do differently if you were starting your business today?

A: We would have a definite attention to the internet—we were into it early because of MCI—and I would have more partners.

Q: What did you do to foster a culture of growth and success in your business?

A: It was unconscious; people were given a lot of responsibility quickly. There was the expectation that we would grow; we always added people. We rarely let anyone go. After passing the threshold of success, we had an anniversary party and gave out recognition to employees.

Q: Did you plan your exit strategy or did it just seem to fall into place?

A: International agencies sought us out. Most of the partners stayed on.

There you have it, from one of the masters:

- Have enough resources going in.
- Hire a publicist—even if you are in the advertising and promotion business.
- Make your company look bigger than it is.
- Become and remain high profile through writing and speaking in your trade or profession.
- Become an earlier adopter of useful technologies, especially for your communications.
- Don't follow the pack.

Smart-Start Summary: Keys for Smart Start Marketing

1. Your marketing is your lifeline to sales. It is a science that can generate measurable results, and you should do everything you can to calculate a ROI on your marketing investments.

By investing the time and the money to properly understand who your customers are, what motivates them, and identifying the media that reach them best, you can attract the kinds of customers who are most likely to buy your products or services.

2. Advertising, promotion, and merchandising all have their unique strengths in your marketing mix, but all of them need to be life-stage gender and culturally appropriate for what may turn out to be a variety of target audiences, all of whom could buy your product.

Older women car purchasers, for example, may respond to an entirely different mix of messages than their similarly aged male counterparts.

3. Emotional connection with your entrepreneurial brand may be even more important to attracting and retaining customers than purely rational benefits you offer.

Remember the Tylenol, Screaming Eagle Cabernet, and Charlie Trotter examples of products that command significantly more business at higher prices than products that are similar in quality but which have less brand value.

4. Retaining loyal customers and using them as net promoters of your business may well be the ultimate secret in developing a Smart-Start start-up.

With a commitment to customer relationship management you can not only attract and retain a loyal, growing customer base, you can transform them into evangelists for your business.

7

Accelerate Your Sales into High Gear

Now that you have analyzed your marketplace and your competitors; determined who your customers are, what they buy, how they buy, when they buy, and where they buy; fine-tuned your selling proposition; and launched a marketing campaign to attract customers, you are ready to engage with your prospects.

Let's face it. No matter how principle-centered and altruistic you are, you didn't go into business for charity; you went into business—or are about to go into business—in order to sell a product or a service. All of the marketing in the world becomes useless if you don't close the sale. Let's focus on what happens next.

Expect to Win, Play to Win

Whether your sales force consists of one person (yourself), a house sales staff, an outsourced team of brokers, a website, or a hired call center, the challenges don't change. This is the acid test. Look to create an extension of your product offerings and your marketing strategy with a congruent sales strategy, one that mirrors what your company stands for. For example, if your augmented product promises extremely quick delivery, your sales team's response time has to deliver with the same speed. Whether this means responding to a cell phone text message right from the trade show floor, maintaining a twenty-four hour call center, or hiring a sales assistant to field the routine inquiries when you or your sales staff leave the building, it makes the difference between winning and losing the sale.

A few years ago, a client of ours decided he wanted to start running a campaign to advertise his new product on several New York City radio stations—starting in three days. We had no script and no commercial recorded yet; plus, we needed to buy the airtime. We felt his father, the semiretired company founder and product developer, would make the best spokesperson. He agreed. Just one problem—his father lived in Florida; his company and our ad agency were in New Jersey, and his father was scheduled to board a plane to Japan in two days.

The next day, we had a script written and approved by the client and had located a studio near the father's home in Florida, sent him the script, and booked the recording session. The other studio shipped the recorded voice tracks to us the next day. We assembled the complete commercial, duplicated it, and shipped it out to all five radio stations. At the same time, we had already checked the audience research, negotiated rates, assembled schedules, gotten them approved, and placed the media buys. Selling equals delivery of a service and delivery on a promise.

Meanwhile, one of the radio stations that should have received a substantial share of the advertising dollar for this campaign did not. During that three-day window when we prepared and placed the ad campaign, this radio station had an off-site meeting. All of its sales and sales management staff were at a hotel with little or no cell service. Their sales assistants back at the studios were not empowered to set rates, and no one picked up their messages from the office until we had already placed the majority of the advertising buys—leaving them a very small share of the revenue. Moral of the story: Protect and grow your sales operation by either maintaining constant customer contact or by having a contingency plan in place, such as setting up pricing in advance of an absence or empowering someone to establish pricing in your absence.

Some Is Better Than None

We should play to win and we should expect to win—but we also need to be flexible enough to meet changing market and competitive needs. None of us compete in a vacuum; we have to understand that our pricing and selling strategies must not only make sense internally, they must also be shaped to meet the realities of your individual competitive environment. As an example, many years ago, a friend married into a family of hoteliers. At one time, his father-in-law enjoyed great success, acquiring thirteen hotel properties and franchises. In time, his empire began to crumble. He hired qualified people, he had good locations, but something went wrong with his selling strategy. When the recently refurbished Ramada Inn just down the road offered its rooms for $69 a night, he refused to lower the rate at his Holiday Inn from its $79 per night. What customer wouldn't gravitate to a spruced-up property for $10 less per night? To them, this amounted to a better value proposition. The result was his competitor ran at 90 percent occupancy; he ran at about 50 percent. Just do the math: with approximately 300 rooms, the Ramada would take in about $6,000 more a night—even though they charged less.

In this case, the only direct cost of goods sold involved the $10 each hotelier paid a chambermaid to make up the room. With a large gross margin, the Holiday Inn owner could easily have met his competitor's price—and even thrown in a free breakfast if necessary in order to keep a customer. That's what successful selling really means—earning and keeping a customer, not just a sale. And sometimes that means aggressively responding to competitive pressure in order to keep that customer as a lifetime purchaser. We counsel our advertising clients to evaluate their campaigns on the basis of the lifelong value of each customer they gain, not just how many people bought once from an ad. Today, with proper data capture, we have the ability to track customer behavior to determine whether or not we have created any measure of loyalty through repeat sales.

A hotel, a restaurant, a cruise ship, an airplane, and even sellers of intangibles like radio or television time all face the same problem. They cannot re-shelve their unsold inventory at the end of the day. The example above of the competing hoteliers gave rise to the likes of Priceline.com, Expedia, Travelocity, and Hotels.com. Today, savvy operators would rather sell every bit of perishable inventory and get something for it than allow any of it to go unsold and get nothing for it. Unlike their counterparts in other industries with a physical inventory, when the day is over, whatever they did not sell they lose.

The key lesson here is to examine your cost of goods and services and determine whether any variation of this approach can enhance your selling strategy. Remember, any marginal revenue above your fixed costs is always to the good.

SALES ADVICE FROM THE REAL TRENCHES: Selling Gravesites

There is little doubt that some products are easier to sell than others. Selling glamorous, luxurious, or fun products that people really want, like BMWs, may have its challenges, but let's face it, the buyers are already interested in your product. There are other products people just don't want to talk about—life insurance comes to mind as a more difficult sell. We're not sure, but among the most difficult products to sell must be cemetery property. If you can sell cemetery property, then you probably have systems and approaches that would be applicable and even more effective with products that are more, shall we say, enlivening.

When we've worked with Denny Sabatini, vice president for large group sales at CMS-Mid-Atlantic, a cemetery management company with cemetery properties in the New York and New Jersey markets, we've always been impressed by his approach. Over the past thirty years, Sabatini has done it all in cemetery sales: door-to-door, cold calling, one-on-one family sales, group presentations. He has also trained and managed hundreds of new sales people, most who have gone on to have very successful careers as well.

So how does Sabatini do it, and what can an entrepreneur learn about selling from a man who specializes in gravesites? Most radically, perhaps, he redefines when a sale occurs. "Everyone teaches that good salespeople practice great customer service, and that great customer service leads to happy customers and additional sales and referrals. I couldn't agree more; I just believe that customer service begins BEFORE THE SALE. In my mind, finding a way to serve a customer, even before he or she buys something from you, is the key to getting a formal purchase." In Sabatini's mind the keys to the success he's had come from a few simple principles:

- **Find ways to serve the customer before you sell the customer.** One of the most powerful things Sabatini does is sincerely try to find ways to serve his potential customers before he brings up any sales issues. "A great opening question in any meeting is to ask, 'How may I serve you? How may I help solve a problem?' By putting himself into a service mode before the sale, he shows his customers just what a relationship with him will be like. After all, if he's this concerned about their issues before they buy they can assume he will be even more concerned after they become customers.

- **Avoid impatience and the temptation of the quick hit.** The greatest barrier to real sales success, according to Sabatini, is the effort to make quick hits. Not that this can't generate real sales, initially. In fact, Sabatini notes that two of the salesmen who used to work for him were great at getting sales on the first meeting—but often in ways that left the customer wondering what had just happened. The sale may have been made, but no trust was generated, no relationship built, no ongoing referral process developed.

- **Face time is key: You have to see them to sell them.** While the Internet and such timesavers as GoToMeeting.com have made it convenient to connect with people over long distances, trust can only be built face to face. According to Sabatini, "So many people want to try to do sales without making the investment in personal meetings. Especially if you are selling large ticket items, personal relationships are key."

- **Sales is sharing enthusiasm for solutions.** If you truly take the perspective of your customer and truly want to solve his problems, when you come up with that solution your enthusiasm will be authentic and contagious. You have done the right thing for your customer, and that generates incredible power and conviction that makes it easy to sell the solution.

- **Create your own growing, powerful, and unpaid sales force.** By taking a service-first approach, Sabatini has created a network of customers who sell for him all the time. As he says, "I used to spend an enormous amount of time cold calling or seeking prospects. Now my customers do that for me. I don't even ask for referrals—they are constantly bringing them to me. And in addition, since I have built a trusted relationship with clearly satisfied customers my trusted relationship precedes me in any new sales situation."

Empowerment: The Key to Your Sales Staff's Success

The world's greatest negotiators, people like Herb Cohen and Roger Dawson, will tell you that everything is negotiable—even when your prospects tell you it isn't. In today's fast-paced, highly competitive world, unless you absolutely own a turf, you need a certain flexibility, especially if your product or service is perceived as a commodity, readily available from someone else for less.

If you don't empower your sales team to make the right call, you lose the sale, and maybe the customer, as well. Several years ago, Barry worked for two different New York City radio stations as an advertising salesperson. The sales cultures differed greatly. At one station, management gave us a range of rates we could use—unless we experienced a sellout. At periods of peak demand, we only sold at the higher end of the range. At the conclusion of the station's highest revenue month, the sales manager congratulated the whole sales staff—and then asked us to think about how much more money each of us would have made if we had charged just 10 percent more per commercial.

At the other station, the local sales manager could not give us rates; only the general sales manager had the authority to set pricing. On at least one occasion when he was unavailable for several hours, we lost sales entirely. In some industries where time is of the essence, you can lose more money by not empowering your people than you would by allowing them to sell at a lower price.

Know When to Hold

Like a poker player, as sellers we have to know when to hold, when to fold, and when to walk away. Not every sale is won or lost on price. And some business contracts or deals are just not worth having.

Knowing when to walk away can make the difference between making money and losing money. For example, years ago, Barry worked for a start-up advertising agency, owned and operated by well-intentioned but inexperienced people. The owners were anxious to cover their growing overhead—maybe too anxious. We presented to a multifranchise auto dealership owned by a wealthy lawyer. He offered us the account, but insisted that we could have it only if we returned half of the media commissions on advertising time and space placements and absorbed all of the creative and production expenses.

The agency took the deal. They should have passed. Even at $1 million of advertising, full commission would have only amounted to $150,000. At half commission, they generated only $75,000. Giving away creative and production is not at zero cost; it's at a negative cost. Giving the client these services at the agency's cost equals zero profit. When all was said and done, the agency earned less than $50,000 on an account that tied up most of its personnel for most of the work week—barely covering their salaries and generating nothing to cover its overhead, let alone zero profit.

SMART-START TIP

How Does My Business Grow?

Become an expert at qualifying prospects and customers. Taking on and keeping only those customers that generate a fair revenue return on your time investment will help you increase your sales and grow your business.

Your sales have to be a win-win, or do not take the deal. When a customer demands too much of your company's selling and servicing resources and does not generate enough revenue for those efforts, you either need to renegotiate your arrangement or move on to customers that will give you a better return on your time investment. Ultimately, your selling depends on your ability to manage your resources—your time, expertise, staff, and products. As your selling skills improve, you will learn how to better ferret out the unproductive customers.

ASK THE EXPERT: Danny Wood, "Sellin' Ain't Just Tellin'"

Danny Wood operates Danny Wood Enterprises, LLC (*www.dwesalesgrowth.com*), a franchised affiliate of the Sandler Sales Institute. He has trained many people from all walks of life in the art of professional selling. He advises business owners to:

- Find a selling system your sales staff can follow.
- Know who your prospects are and qualify them.
- Determine the reasons for doing business with your prospects.
- Develop a plan for determining how to contact your prospects (networking, cold calling, e-mail).
- Develop a prospecting plan based on that.
- Get sales training. It provides a safe environment where you can grow.
- Don't look for a quick fix.
- Prepare for rejection and rebound from it.

Some frequent selling mistakes to avoid are:

- Continuing to follow up with poor prospects
- Making your pitch before finding out if your prospect can afford your product or service
- Making your pitch before finding out what the prospect's process is for making a decision

Much has changed in sales. What worked in the past often will not work today and going forward in the future.

Let's explore how we need to adapt in order to see our sales grow. Some points of difference are:

- In the past, people sold features and benefits.
- Now, gaining trust and overcoming past bad experiences ranks at the top of the list.
- Today, we need to build relationships and achieve a comfort level with the prospect.
- Now, prospects want to know how much you care.

Use technology to your advantage—get database software to manage your contacts. However, technology does not replace face-to-face contact.

How Does Your Sales Network Grow?

Everyone has a sales network; some of us just don't realize it. We surround ourselves with friends, family, colleagues, suppliers, mentors—people we remain connected to. How strong is your network? Perhaps the real test is at a time of need. If you ever lost a job through a downsizing or layoff, you probably began to tap into your network for support and to secure a new position. As an entrepreneur, your network serves to support your start-up, to nurture your growing enterprise, and to continue vesting that growth. One key theme throughout this book is clear: Successful entrepreneurs surround themselves with teams of experts in the disciplines where they lack expertise. In the new world of sales, networking and partnering is key to entrepreneurial sales success.

Ted Fattoross, founder of the 1,200 member Network Plus organization, provides some expert tips (*www.joinnetworkplus. com*). Fattoross believes in a simple philosophy: "We're taught as children not to talk to strangers, but that's exactly what we have to unlearn." Fattoross, a successful public speaker, refers to the six degrees of separation between you and the person you want to meet. All you have to do is learn to connect the dots.

Successful networkers like Fattoross know that, in its simplest form, productive networking requires you to do two things:

a. Give first.
b. Ask for what you need.

In order to serve others, you first need to develop a wide and deep Rolodex. Become the go-to gal, the one everyone calls when they need a referral for any service, because they know that if it came from you, it's got to be good.

Who Knows You?

Barry remembers a good example of how this can work. Rich was a sales person who seemed to know everybody. More importantly, to borrow another phrase from Fattoross, it's really about who knows you—and everybody knew Rich. This didn't happen by accident. Before the sign went up at any new retail establishment, Rich was in there. By the time the sign went up, he had the order for the new establishment's radio advertising, before the newspapers or the cable TV reps. You see, Rich had his spotters out there—people watching out for him and tipping him off as soon as they saw the crews working around that new establishment—and he always made sure that he provided networking help back to the folks who helped him.

A way to go beyond traditional networking is to form strategic alliances with companies who have aligned business interests. For example, in one of Michael's businesses he licensed the first spelling-correction software to companies who sold word processors. The word processor companies were excited to incorporate the spelling software as a differentiating benefit that increased the popularity and sales success of their own word processors. In this case, Michael's company never had to hire any salespeople—his strategic partners' sales forces sold all his products for him, at an extraordinarily profitable level for his company and his strategic partners.

Do Unto Others

When thinking about sales networking and strategic partnering, remember the golden rule: People want to work with people who do the right thing. For example, some time ago Barry worked with a gentleman on the launch of a new diet product. The company he worked for made promises and never kept them. He succeeded in getting the product into a major drugstore chain, but his company never ran the advertising they promised. His reputation and career were more important than a job. He left the company—and the industry—and took a job outside of his career field. But he had developed a trusted relationship with many folks who respected his integrity, and Barry and others helped him get his next job and return to the industry he knew and loved. People give business to people they know and trust, who have opened doors to them, who have proven their integrity. Sales networking is the real thing, and in this millennium working with strategic partners and networkers may be the ultimate sales secret.

NETWORKING TIPS FOR EVERYDAY

To take your networking skills to the highest level possible, put these practices into action:

- **Make it a lifestyle**—Talk to everyone, at every station in life. He's just a drycleaner? He may be cleaning your top prospect's suits.
- **Give first**—Find out what other people need and fulfill their needs—without expecting a direct return. Someone else will pay you back another day.
- **Fill your Rolodex**—In order to become a referral source, you first have to build a vast database. Get to know a lot of people. Become the go-to guy that people trust as a resource for quality people.
- **Ask for what you need**—Not everyone you meet will need you or your services. You want to do business with the people they know, with their Rolodex. When you help people get what they want and you ask for what you need, they feel obligated but not hunted. They will reciprocate and refer in return.
- **Engage with people**—Become involved with your prospect's favorite charity or cause célèbre; invite them into your circle. It beats the pants off of e-mailing them proposals and packages. They might even take your next call.
- **You can't fake sincerity**—In all you do, be genuine. Sincerity rises to the top. Treat your prospects and clients as important people first, professionals next, as a meal ticket last.
- **Form strategic alliances**—Align yourself with people who are in a position to feed you continuous leads. Ask yourself who calls on a similar profile of decision makers yet is not your competitor. It may be the printer or web designer that calls on the marketing directors you want to do business with. Just remember, share is a verb as well as a noun.

Technology and Sales in the 21st Century

For the 21st century entrepreneur the world is wildly different, and in some ways easier, than it was just ten years ago. Technology like the Internet, which didn't exist in any consumer viable way even ten years ago, is now so pervasive and so powerful that it can accelerate and assist your start-up venture in ways that were previously unthinkable. A combination of new technologies has made it possible to do many things on your own or with virtual partners faster and at far lower costs than ever before. These technologies have also brought down barriers to entry and made markets and opportunities that were previously protected available to the creative entrepreneur.

We talk about things like ways to create virtual partners for almost every aspect of your business, including shipping, administration, inventory, and production later in the book. But one technology is so overwhelmingly powerful and useful in a start-up that it deserves special attention: the Internet.

The Internet: The Great Equalizer

Perhaps no other technology has had and continues to have such profound effects on the way we do business than the Internet. In a short period of time the Internet has gone from a fad that generated clicks instead of sales to a tool that can allow an entrepreneur to start a business and market products faster and at lower risks than ever before in history. Ultimately, what the Internet is doing is removing the middleman from our transactions. And without middlemen, we can decide to take our products or business services directly to the consumer, in effect, leveling the playing field for players of all sizes. To give you an example what a revolution the Internet has created, we look not at *BusinessWeek* or *Forbes*, but instead at *Rolling Stone*, the Bible of the music industry. And our revolutionary entrepreneurs are a UK rock band called Radiohead. We're not putting too fine a point on this. As *Rolling Stone*'s cover proclaims: The

Future Belongs to Radiohead. Not because of their music, but because of the way they are using the Internet to explode the classic music-industry business model. Radiohead has recently done the unthinkable—broken from their well-established label and decided to take complete control of their music, not just through copyright ownership, but in the way it is marketed, distributed, priced, and sold.

For their most recent album, *Rainbows*, Radiohead created downloads on their website. They marketed this through websites, PR, and fan-website links. They are pricing the downloads from free to $212. And according to *Rolling Stone*'s article, which quotes com-Score, "a significant percentage" of the 1.2 million visitors to the website downloaded the album. Again, according to the *Rolling Stone* article, the payer averaged about $6 per download, which, factoring in people who paid nothing, generated the band about $2.26 per album. This is more than they would receive from their record label deal. Because they are not creating typical CDs, they need no inventory, warehouses, or shipping capabilities. They don't even need any employees to take orders—they can do everything by bank credit card or PayPal systems.

The Internet is essential to giving you a competitive advantage; it is the slingshot in your David's arsenal against the well-established Goliaths of the business world. Whether your business can use every aspect of the Internet the way Radiohead does, you need to use as many aspects of it as you can. If nothing else, you need to create an attractive website that gives your customers the information about you they need when they need it. Consumers are still struck by first impressions, and for many of them your website can create a great and very positive impression, and for very little money. In fact, because of the proliferation of web development tools, websites that might have cost thousands of dollars just five years ago can be created for hundreds by skilled web developers. These web experts can also help you incorporate the basics of Search Engine Optimization

(SEO) into your site so customers who need your products can find you.

CEO Space: Brainstorming for Entrepreneurs

Imagine if someone took many of the best practices in entre- preneurship, tapped a great collection of experienced busi- ness minds, and combined them into an intense training course . . . and added super networking to that. Someone did. Meet B.J. Dohrmann, creator of CEO Space, an innovative business incubator that at some time may be right for your firm (*www .ceospace.net*). Dohrmann, a two-time New York Times best-sell- ing author (*Money Magic and Perfection Can be Had, Redemption: the Co-operation Revolution*), explains what led to this training program:

"A dark hole existed in the entrepreneur window for solid information about the sequence of events necessary to succeed. A training program was missing. The resulting success story has become a legend. Last year, CEO Space fostered the release of the best consumer electronics product, the leading independent film, the best pet product, and a host of other winning business launches. CEO Space's process reduces risk, lowers the capi- tal outlay and the time frame to reach the business's goals and objectives."

How did they construct the model? "We developed a group of the leading trainers from Fortune 100 companies; we spent three years doing it in the late 1980s. The model includes an intense trade show." The trade show, combined with highly focused workshops conducted by the world's leading experts in manufacturing, marketing, and financing, also adds on-the- spot networking opportunities with high-level, well-connected achievers that can jumpstart virtually any enterprise with insights and connections that most entrepreneurs never have access to.

Who Can Best Benefit from CEO Space?

An existing business, three to fifteen years in place, looking to step into hyper growth and increase their resale value by multiples. According to Dohrmann, the single most important difference between those enterprises that achieve great success and those that do not is, "Most businesses have a weak plan and a weak team to execute. The brand strategy drives the products. You need the experts to create the right sequences so you have the resources to reach earnings targets, rather than putting your early stage growth into survival mechanics."

Smart-Start Summary: Keys to Smart-Start Sales

1. Develop a sales plan with clear-cut objectives and a strategy to achieve them.
2. Invest in training your sales force for optimal results.
3. Understand the relational aspects of selling, which trump the transactional aspects.
4. Under-promise and over-deliver to your customers.
5. Understand the life-long value and referral potential of each customer.
6. Learn to become a master networker and turn strategic partners into your hidden sales weapon.
7. Investigate how the Internet can be your key to fast, immediate, and trackable sales.

8

New Ways to Manage People, Systems, and Support Systems

As a start-up focused on getting your business up and running, having the right people to help is key. Many companies say that their most important assets are their people. For start-ups, where every employee has a disproportionate impact on your success, this concept is even more important than for large, established firms. As we have indicated, you and your company are only as good as your people. That said, your people are only as good as their productivity level—both the quantity and the quality of their output and their interfaces with the company, its suppliers, and its customers. Yes, hire the best people you can afford, but take out some insurance on retaining them, by adopting regular training. Loyal employees, are the absolute key to attracting loyal customers. At the onset, your business may be small enough to conduct your own training. In time as your workforce expands you may need to invest in hiring professional trainers. In its 2007 "State of the Industry Report," the American Society of Training and Development (*www.astd.org*) indicated an average of $1,040 per employee was spent in 2006 on direct training expenses—with an estimated additional $795 per employee for indirect expenses including travel, work-time lost, and learning-event fees. This only represents 2.33 percent of payroll—less than most businesses devote to other expenditures. The report shows an average of 44.3 hours per employee devoted annually to training. How much of a difference can that make? We asked those who do it every day.

LMI: Performance, Productivity, and Profit

In 1964, then twenty-seven-year-old Paul J. Meyer had earned $1 million by selling life insurance. He wanted to train other people to achieve the kind of success he enjoyed, so he founded LMI, Leadership Management Incorporated (*www.lmi-usa.com*). Forty-three years later, his vision continues to manifest itself in the worldwide training company he founded. Today, Tony

Stigliano trains the franchise owners on how to become successful business operators themselves as they seek to train other business owners in critical functions like sales, communication skills, and time management. We asked Stigliano what to look for when seeking a professional training program for yourself and your staff.

First and foremost, the process must be duplicated for every person you hire. Businesses so often go about selling and forget about their marketing and customer service. Here are some important basics for your training program:

- It starts with your hiring process for employees. You must profile them in order to determine if there is a fit for both the position and the organization.
- Next, they must understand your vision, mission, and purpose—and everyone must buy into it. They must understand the types of customers they deal with and what approaches work—both positive and negative. Every employee must understand the importance of keeping the customer happy. It's the KLT Process: Know, like, trust. Use it, and customers will stay with you.
- An important component of your training program should include how you promote your business in the community—you must develop a marketing plan the employees participate in. You need to address the safety, administrative, and cooperation issues that apply to your business.
- You must include sales training to get people to see why they need your product.

What impact does all of this have on your enterprise? Simply put, it results in increased productivity. Proper training will improve employees' behavior, attitude, long-term relationships with customers, and retention, and ultimately, that spells increased profitability. Stigliano points out, "Too often, people hire employees based on knowledge and skills; however, they let people go based on attitude. Rather than letting them go, train them. People don't do things because they either don't want to or they don't know how to."

Training must be an ongoing process. Schools use repetition and all the senses to teach. It takes time. Stigliano recommends the same person should remain in place to facilitate and review your training even if different people conduct the actual trainings.

Few people understand peoples' personalities. You need a process based on past successes, with testing, to duplicate past successes. Business owners need to reduce overhead. Employee turnover and retraining, at any level, costs your business. Training becomes a critical function, even with minimum-wage people.

Technology is critical today. People want quick service. People buy differently today. You must understand why they want to buy. Your initial customer contact person can make or break a new customer. They must have honesty, integrity, and good communication with your clients. They must understand the global side of it—they will encounter more than one type of customer; one size does not fit all. Don't sell what the customer doesn't need. Stigliano advises considering a drip-marketing program in which you send out small bits of information regularly.

Evaluating Training Programs

Stigliano advises the following when considering a training program:

- Do three to four short-term trials.
- Look for people to talk to about their results—clients the training company worked with.
- Interview the training company as if you were hiring them.
  - Ask yourself if they are trying to sell you or help you.
  - They should guarantee some measurable results.
  - Ask them how they will show you a ROI.

◆ Examine their methodology—does the program include a multisensory approach, spaced repetition, clear goals, and actions steps?

What does the future of training look like? According to Stigliano, we will see more web-based training in addition to facilitation. The ASTD's "2007 State of the Industry Report," referenced earlier, bears this out, with over 30 percent of training hours now devoted to technology-based learning, while live instructor-lead delivery declines.

Stigliano describes the important difference between training and development. Training is informational (it usually takes only one to three days). Most often, people go back to the way they were after completing it. Development, on the other hand, produces results and applications that are measured.

The Accidental Trainer

Art Suriano, CEO of Total Sound Infotainment, *www.total-soundinfo.com*, was educated as a musician, previously served as an ad agency principal, and later became a product developer with an innovative audio direct-mail program known as Talking Mail. Today, his company creates training programs used by major retail chains for their associates. What lead him to enter the training arena? Suriano confides that it happened completely by accident. He started his company to produce the familiar in-store radio announcements so often heard at supermarkets and other retail stores. A client expressed an interest in what could be done for his employees, rather than for his customers. Total Sound developed a before-and-after-hours radio program for the employees of Stern's Department Stores. Then, they produced similar programs for other sister store chains within the Federated family of stores. Customer service improved dramatically during that period, in part due to the new training programs.

Barnes & Noble then gave Suriano's company a chance to do on-floor training. Eventually, they began to work with

Linens and Things, doing product-knowledge training. These modules consisted of audio learning delivered by headsets, while the employees stood in front of the store shelves. Total Sound dubbed their programs "L" training (logical training), and helped their retail store customers get them paid for by the vendors, who had a vested interest in selling more of their products.

The programs resulted in high levels of knowledge retention. In spite of this, many companies' training departments wanted online training. The advantage to Total Sound's programs? Suriano explains that they kept people on the selling floor, while other programs took employees off of the floor, then they had to go back on the floor. Total Sound's training solution is a learn-by-doing process.

Assessing the Impact of Your Training

Always look for the acid test. Total Sound's most successful program involved a contract with a conglomerate of several retail music and entertainment store chains. They selected a control group of sixty out of the 1,400 stores. They conducted both a customer service and two product knowledge programs for a period of thirty days. The stores that participated in the training were outselling the others four to one. Why does it work? Suriano explains that "L" training combines the auditory, visual, tactile, and kinesthetic—the employee learns by doing while watching and listening. Plus, the programs are entertaining. Total Sound's newest generation of programs, known as "4L," have the employee learn on the computer first, then conduct some physical activity on the selling floor then, return to a CD then finally test and score the test.

Total Sound's CEO indicates that over $70 billion are spent annually on training, yet less than 10 percent of that is proven to be effective. As a smart-start entrepreneur, you can't afford that. What else accounts for the low return on investment? Art relates, "Ineffective programs; programs that are too complex, that are boring, that are too detailed and that are too time consuming."

So, how do you evaluate a potential training program? Suriano offers these tips:

- Today, we've become scanners, not readers. Just tell them what they need to know.
- Don't take a part timer and overdo training.
- Go to your top vendors and ask for training money. Show them the program. Often, they will support it.
- Don't get taken in by flashy programs.

Instead, contact the training company's references. Talk to someone who can give you actual performance feedback on the program they ran (not the training manager). Be sure you understand both the methodologies and the delivery systems of the training. Most importantly, ask what the objective of the program was and how the company delivered against it.

Develop Yourself

We are all works in progress. In both our personal lives and as business people, we must continue evolving and developing. While the entrepreneur needs to train his or her people in the functional aspects of the enterprise, we contribute to ourselves and our business success by committing to our own personal growth, as well. One of the most successful entrepreneurs we've worked with is Ed Shackelford, who founded a start-up twenty years ago that now sells over $1 billion in insurance per year. Ed didn't go to college, but he has grown on a personal and business level by reading developmental and inspirational authors like John Maxwell, or Napoleon Hill, or Og Mandino, every morning. And according to Ed, that's been a key to his success. His personal commitment to self-improvement has allowed him to learn about new approaches, keep open to change, and give the appropriate value to the contributions of his team.

Dr. John De Martini has addressed millions of people worldwide on tapping into their own potential and releasing their own greatness (*www.DrDemartini.com*).

What makes the difference between entrepreneurs who are just okay, those that are great, and those that are spectacular? De Martini explains, "It's how their goals, their ambitions, and their vision align to their highest values. Nobody has to get you up to do what is highest on your value hierarchy. You are inspired from within. You require motivation from outside for your lowest values. When an entrepreneur is congruent with his or her highest values, nothing will stop them—it's their own calling and destiny to get it done. We develop inertia, hesitation, and procrastination around things that are low on our values."

What is the single most important attribute a start-up businessperson needs in order to succeed? According to De Martini, they truly have something—a product, service, or idea communicated in such a way that people can't wait to get it. It must be communicated in the hierarchy of the highest values of those people they want to serve. You can't wait to get up in the morning to give your service; they can't wait to get your service throughout the world.

Can anyone genuinely succeed in business if she is not principle centered? DeMartini says, "I define success as actions being congruent with our own values. People can tell when you're not congruent. When I speak, people know this is thirty-five years of dedication. That sells. You can't fake that. I am a retired doctor. Patients can tell if you're with them. The market can sense authenticity. When you go into a company, if the people are inspired and enthusiastic and grateful for their jobs the company is going places. People are never dedicated to a company; they are dedicated to their values. If they feel they can fulfill their values in the context of the company, they are electrified."

"I make myself accountable to my checklist. I ask what worked and what didn't. How can I do what I'm doing more effectively? How did whatever happen support or serve me?

Quarterly, write out everything you do, prioritize it according to productivity, purposefulness, profitability, time spent; delegate lower priority things and get on to doing the highest priority things.

"Don't allow idle time; schedule your agenda for the day. Fill it with what you want before it becomes filled with what you don't. For example, when I was in practice, I had a list for my down time—I read biographies of great leaders; I wrote thank yous to clients. Every day I read from a book of everything that inspires me."

"A business plan rules out fantasies, delusions, and whims; things that won't work in the marketplace. Make sure the person has the value system congruent with that entrepreneurial venture. When people grow up perceiving they were challenged, they became courageous. Those looking for ease don't make good entrepreneurs. Overprotection and support do not challenge stagnant belief systems."

"If you need financial expertise, get someone ten times bigger than the vision you have for your company. Association: surround yourself with people that are living the magnitude of your vision and beyond."

"Identify leaders in fields similar to yours; identify the traits that make those great entrepreneurs; ask yourself, Where do I have those traits? and wake them up. We deny what we have inside; we minimize it. Use others to reflect that."

What does De Martini believe is the single most important skill that every entrepreneur needs to master in order to achieve extreme success? (Pay careful attention to the answer.)

"The ability to communicate their inspired vision of service to the people they are going to sell to and to enroll on their team. Make it clear and enthusiastically communicate it to others."

The message comes through loudly and clearly. Determine what you stand for. Define whom you serve. Determine what they value most. Communicate how your service fulfills their values. Sounds like the makings of successful marketing, doesn't it? It all starts with investing in your people, which begins with committing to your own personal growth and development.

Managing and Leading Your People in a Regulated World

Let us congratulate you again on your decision to go into business for yourself. Taking control of your life ranks high on the list of noble pursuits. However, the moment you decided to hire employees you just lost control. To an extent, the regulatory agencies have now taken control of your business. Pay careful attention to this section. You will need it in order to navigate the minefields you just entered.

Of all the assets that create value in your business, your human resources top the list. At the same time, they can derail your enterprise if you do not manage them properly. All the proprietary technologies, systems, and products in the world will not rocket your business to the top without the right people following your lead. Plain and simple, many start-ups fail because far too much of the enterprise rests with the founders. Unless and until the founders begin to delegate the company's workload, its growth becomes stunted. As a breed, entrepreneurs often fail in this respect. They may make great product developers, salespeople, etc., but if they cannot create an organization, communicate their vision, and allow others to carry out their mission, their businesses will not grow.

Every one of us that ever started a business—in any industry, with any amount of money, of any size—soon faced the need to let go. When the moment arrives where you find yourself performing too many functions, spending too much time, not experiencing growth, and most of all, performing unproductive jobs that really don't help your business grow, you need to start hiring help. My dear friend and mentor, business coach and trainer Terry Viney, always talks about working on high-payoff activities. You don't send Rembrandt to paint the barn, so to speak. In plain English, if you can hire someone else to perform a function that frees you up to perform another function that will produce a greater return to your business on that time investment, then find the funds to do it.

Do you have to break the bank to begin hiring? Certainly not. In the beginning, if your enterprise is not cash rich, look for alternatives to traditional hiring. For example, don't overlook hiring student interns. Nearby colleges and trade or technical schools may have sharp undergraduates that will benefit by gaining practical experience in your business, along with earning course credit for their work in your company. They may even become regular employees after graduation. Depending on the type of work needed, you may even tap into the resources of a sheltered workshop for the handicapped. Often, these organizations have people ready, willing, and able to work. At the same time, your company will develop goodwill by giving back to the community. In both of the above cases, you will probably find highly motivated workers that will work for relatively modest wages. Finally, in today's world there are numerous displaced workers with high skill levels that have been downsized or otherwise forced out of jobs, just waiting for an opportunity. Grab them.

About fifteen years ago, an entirely new concept in hiring appeared. Known as employee leasing companies, these agencies offered businesses the opportunity to access and hire a pre-screened talent pool without having to perform all of the payroll and administrative functions themselves. Advertising for these firms enticed employers to use their services, telling them to "fire their employees and lease them back from us." In today's world flexibility becomes the key to success for many start-ups. The fewer the obligations, the more the company can focus on growing and servicing its customer base. Outsourcing administrative functions like hiring, payroll, and benefits will help the fledgling entrepreneurial company ensure itself against distracting details as well as some of the regulatory morass we will discuss in this chapter.

We said earlier the minute you begin hiring employees, your life and your company's will change dramatically. We all operate our businesses in a heavily regulated and highly litigious society. You will face many hot-button issues once you begin hiring employees. Most start-ups cannot afford to hire a full-time human resources person to navigate the minefields. The first step involves becoming aware of the issues. So, how do you handle it? The best alternative to a qualified on-staff human resources director involves engaging the services of an outsourced HR consultant or working with a firm like Administaff, which provides a menu of services for start-up companies including a virtual human resources department.

These companies can keep you out of trouble by ensuring you have some of the basics covered without incurring the cost of the typically high salary and benefits a qualified staff member would demand. A good HR consultant will help you draft employee manuals, policies, and procedures that will stand up to the scrutiny of judges and lawmakers. Many HR consultants previously served as HR directors at larger companies. Firms like Administaff will already have standard policy manuals in place for you to use. In either case use professionals here, because the laws are constantly changing and personnel issues are serious business. Just some of the beliefs you may have to change include the following.

I Can Hire Anyone I Want, Can't I?

I can hire people just like me: Nobody too old, nobody too young, nobody handicapped, nobody from a foreign country, and only people who attend my church, right? At its most basic, the U.S Equal Employment Opportunity Act states that you cannot discriminate in the hiring, firing, or promotion of employees based on age, gender, race, religion, national origin, handicap, and more recently, sexual orientation. Let's be clear: there are no exceptions. Some states have enacted their own laws in addition to the federal statute. That means showing undue preference to an employee or a prospective hire over someone equally or better qualified, on the basis of one of the above factors, can result in the filing of a complaint against you with the Equal Employment Opportunity Commission (EEOC) as well as a possible lawsuit.

A New Jersey court upheld a claim of reverse discrimination by a twenty-five-year-old bank vice president that claimed the bank tried to pressure him into resigning after hiring him. Management feared embarrassment if other employees learned they hired such a young person at a high salary. The court said no can do. While the burden of proof may rest with the accuser, such complaints can strangle you with red tape and detract significantly from running your enterprise. It's simply not worth it. Watch your practices and those of your employees.

I Can Fire Anyone I Want, Can't I?

After all, it's my business, isn't it? Although some states discourage labor unions and are designated so-called right-to-work states, the term "at-will employment" still does not guarantee you the right to terminate an employee without cause. Make sure you document the actions leading up to your decision to terminate—such as keeping notes from meetings, issuing letters of warning, conducting written performance appraisals the employee initials to acknowledge receipt, etc. With the exception of totally frivolous claims, anyone engaging a good labor attorney can still bring charges against you. Ensure yourself and your company against the agony, lost productivity, and legal costs of a wrongful termination suit by clearly spelling out performance standards for each and every employee with their job descriptions.

I Can Get Real Close to My Employees, Can't I?

In recent years, several states have enacted very chilling statutes to curtail sexual harassment. Even churches and nonprofits need to concern themselves with this one, in the wake of allegations of abuses by clergy. The essence of these laws is that an employer may not allow any employee, including the owner, and in many cases, even outside contractors, to make any unwanted advances toward any employee. For many years before these laws existed, employers would use their position and power to exact sexual favors from employees that complied, fearing loss of their jobs.

Some of the laws, such as the New Jersey statute, broaden the definition of harassment to include creating a hostile work environment. The definition of this practice? If you hang pictures of scantily clad women, use abusive language, tell lewd jokes, or otherwise encourage employees to behave in a manner that fosters discomfort you have created a hostile work environment. It is actionable, so ensure yourself by cleaning up your workplace.

So, what happens when employees begin to date one another? How do you determine if the advance was unwanted or if it was invited and welcomed? Especially if one employee supervises the other, you have a potential bombshell on your hands. Can you enforce a no-fraternization policy after hours, off premises? What about the company Christmas party, when someone consumes too much alcohol? Are you responsible for what happens? Yes. If it's a company-sponsored or company-sanctioned function, in most cases you will be held responsible for your employees' behavior. Take steps to ensure yourself against these problems with an enforceable employee code of conduct in your handbook or manual, given to all new hires at the commencement of their employment.

A supplement to the *New Jersey Law Journal* on employment law carried a story cautioning attorneys that "Law Firms Aren't Exempt from Employment Laws." It cited the case of a Boston-area law firm that agreed to pay five former employees who claimed they were exposed to race and sex harassment. In addition, the firm had to adopt a policy acceptable to the EEOC as well as provide sexual-harassment training immediately.

I Can Tell My Employees What to Wear to Work, Can't I?

Dress codes present an extremely tricky area. At best, you have to hope employees will use good sense. Many company's dress-code policies simply will not hold up in a court of law. Except where uniforms are required, while you can specify certain attire as appropriate or at least preferred, good taste in clothing and grooming is subjective and employees can and will often challenge your standards successfully. Check out these two employer faux-pas.

In 2005, *Radio Ink* magazine reported a story originally appearing on MSNBC concerning a former radio sales representative working for Viacom, the parent company of CBS. Shawn Brooks, from a family of mixed race, challenged his supervisors for distributing a book entitled *New Dress for Success* (John T. Molloy, 2001). The book advised that African Americans selling to Caucasians should not wear Afro hairstyles or African-style clothing. It also advised Hispanics not to use hair tonics that would give a greasy or shiny look, to avoid triggering a negative reaction. The end result: a $600,000 award to the former employee.

Big companies should know better, right? They usually have in-house counsel to review policies before management distributes them throughout the company, right? Well, a major New York City bank issued a staff memorandum on its new casual dress policy, over the signature of its chairman and chief executive officer. It detailed what items of clothing qualified as appropriate or inappropriate. Just one problem: It mentioned dress sandals (for women) as appropriate; it states that sandals (for men) are inappropriate. While it may qualify as good taste, the policy, if challenged, would not hold up. As it was written, it is discriminatory. When it comes to employment law, for the most part, what is good for the goose is good for the gander.

I Can Tell My Employees For Whom to Vote, Can't I?

The government, as the guardian of standards, has to police its own house first. Many years ago, the Hatch Act was written to prevent Federal Employees from mixing politics with the business of government. Hence, your supervisor could not exert pressure on you to support his favorite candidate for office. Partisan politics were forbidden in the government workplace. While private industry has not always been held to as stringent a standard, wisdom dictates keeping your politics out of the workplace. Employees have the right to their own political affiliations, even if they differ from their employer's.

Nothing Controversial Goes on the Bulletin Board or Gets Circulated Without My Approval, Right?

Free-speech issues in the workplace will also present challenges. Even more than dress codes, telling employees what they can read, watch, or listen to, provided it doesn't interfere with the performance of their work or offend their coworkers, is difficult at best. Preventing them from circulating opinions that differ from yours presents a minefield unto itself. Remember, when you deal with constitutional issues, you deal with the supreme law of the land. You may not like the slogan on the bumper sticker, the imprint on the T-shirt, or the flier on the bulletin board, but avoid heavy handedness that could cost you.

Exception: You have every right to forbid employees from soliciting for money or selling products or services on company time and premises. This causes people to feel obligated, and can result in disputes you should not have to resolve.

Guns and Knives at the Workplace?

When it comes to workplace violence, zero tolerance is the only answer. If anyone gets hurt, you will most certainly be caught in the midst of it when the lawsuits start flying. You have every right to forbid employees from bringing firearms and other dangerous weapons to your workplace. Going up to the hunting cabin? Stop home first. Even an accident will result in a disaster for your business. Violent employees have no place in your workplace. Check to see if your health insurance plan has an intervention program at the first sign of an outbreak of employee violence. Many plans cover psychotherapy under Employee Assistance Programs (EAPs). Clearly communicate the zero-tolerance policy from day one.

I'm Not Responsible for Accidents, Am I?

Every employer has an obligation to provide a safe workplace. It took a long time before government actually enacted formal protections for work-related illnesses and injuries. Many states require employers to carry mandatory workers' compensation insurance. Moreover, the Occupational Safety and Health Administration (OSHA) will spot-check companies from time to time—often without warning. Correct unsafe conditions; they will cost you more in the long run than you can imagine, from lost productivity to disability payments to workers' compensation claims. In this regard, the law will cut you very little slack.

I Can Put Anything I Want into Their Contracts, Can't I?

Employment contracts have to stand up to rigorous tests. Ensuring them requires professional help. As much as you would like them to stay loyal to you, people have the right to pursue employment—or entrepreneurship—elsewhere. Many noncompete clauses have not held up in court. Why? The courts have ruled, by and large, that you can't prevent a person from engaging in their chosen profession or occupation. While your contract may prevent them from soliciting your customers, you can't force them out of your industry.

In an ideal world, where money is not an issue, hire a qualified human resources director on staff to create policy and ensure compliance. In the real world of business start-ups, consider engaging the services of an outsourced human resources consultant. At the very least, if this still proves cost prohibitive you can subscribe to services that issue prewritten manuals and policies already created and reviewed by professionals. Some of these are offered by payroll companies such as HR Comply from *www.powerpay.com*; others are available from online services like Business 21 Publishing (request information from *www.hr training@b21pubs.com*).

In its most extreme form, employer abuses have far-reaching effects. A few years back, an advertising sales representative from a major financial publication became embroiled in a dispute with his employer. Ironically, the employer attempted to fire the salesman for abusing his expense account. In court papers filed in the State of New York, the employee alleged that he was ordered by his supervisors to procure both strippers and large quantities of alcohol at a hotel conference center, charge these items to his company expense account, and report them as sports and show tickets given to clients. The company did not deny the allegations in their answer and counterclaim. Furthermore, the employee reported that the publication's management, at its highest levels, requested him to procure a luxury car for his superiors' personal use shortly before a favorable review of that automobile appeared in the publication. The case appeared on Court TV.

Let's put this one under the microscope. First and foremost, the company created a hostile work environment, leaving itself open to possible harassment suits by female employees, by procuring lewd entertainment at a company-sponsored event. Second, management coerced the employee into misusing funds at a publicly traded company, leaving itself open to potential shareholder action and a Securities and Exchange investigation. Third, the company left itself vulnerable to a wrongful termination suit. Ultimately, both parties withdrew their claims after incurring substantial legal fees. Start-ups beware: discretion rules!

PROTECT YOURSELF AND YOUR ENTERPRISE . . .

The old adage about an ounce of prevention being worth a pound of cure proves truer in the area of personnel management than anywhere else. Theodore Williams, vice president of Centaur Consulting (*www.centaurconsultinginc.com*), offers the critical must haves for any start-up's employee handbook. Protect your start-up by including these items:

- A statement indicating that the person's employment is "at will." This establishes that the term of employment is not guaranteed or permanent.
- A policy statement on discrimination and sexual harassment. This alerts the employee to the unacceptability of such conduct.
- A progressive discipline policy outlining the stages: verbal warnings, written warnings, termination. This policy should also indicate that the use of drugs or alcohol as well as theft or violence is grounds for immediate termination.
- A statement of employee benefits including that they are subject to change by the company.
- A dress code that is appropriate to the job the employee is performing. Keep it as generic as possible.
- A statement of work hours and overtime policy that clearly indicates how it is paid as well as who is exempt.
- A policy on military leave for reservists.
- A sick leave and bereavement policy as well as a jury-duty policy indicating how the company will pay employees for such time off. (Typically, the employer can offer three days, but can extend it for special situations.)
- A Family Medical Leave Act policy covering the employee's absence in cases of illness of immediate family members.

- A policy covering court leave (paid or unpaid) when an employee must serve as a witness. Williams recommends treating it like jury duty.
- A policy governing maternity and paternity leave and adoption. Williams cautions that many people now seek to adopt foreign children, which may result in an extended employee absence. Be reasonable and flexible, but spell out the policy in advance.
- A policy regarding non-competes. This is most critical if your company has proprietary intellectual property and an employee wants to leave and go to work for a competitor. Williams advises you simply state you have such a policy in the handbook and present the actual policy at the time of the final interview, when you hire the employee. Presenting an onerous non-compete document after the employee has accepted your offer and has turned down other offers could weaken your claim if the employee later leaves and challenges your policy. Williams advises you check the legality of your policy with an employment attorney.
- A statement that the company conducts annual performance reviews. This helps you justify your decision to remove or retain an employee.
- A compensation policy should appear stating that increases are performance related and based on the profitability of the company.

Pay Your Taxes or You Will Be Working for the State

We know from personal experience the pain of paying the many bills it takes to run a business. Like it or not, the government does have first priority. Before Barry took over the management of a Virginia radio station with an absentee owner, his predecessor had neglected to send in the payroll taxes. Bad move. He had to beg the owner to bring these payments up to date. Here's the priority order for paying your bills:

- **Pay your employees first**. No exceptions. If your payroll is late and your employees report you to your state's Wage and Hour Board, they can place liens on your accounts.
- **Payroll taxes come next**. You must make the employer contributions for Social Security, Unemployment, etc., as you pay out the wages.
- **Sales tax**. If your state requires it, they often require payment when you charge it, not when you collect it.
- **Income tax**. At least you can report and send this in quarterly if you operate as a corporation. One of the benefits to organizing a start-up as an LLC is that for tax purposes your company is treated like a partnership. You only have to pay income taxes at the end of the year, and the income is taxed as a pass-through on the personal income of the members or partners.

Now, you can pay the rent, the utilities, and your suppliers. A former Internal Revenue Service agent once advised a group of us taking a small business management course to file a tax return, file it on time, and send in something—even $1. By doing so, you will avoid the three most common mistakes and violations: failure to file, late filing, and failure to pay. By covering yourself this way, the government can only charge you with penalties and interest on any unpaid balance of taxes you owe.

Don't look for loopholes. A small company involved in checking doctors' credentials for health insurers thought they could avoid paying payroll taxes by turning their staff into independent contractors. We had a Certified Public Accountant warn them against the practice; we secured a copy of the IRS publication defining the difference between employees and contractors. They insisted on doing it anyway, losing staff members in the process. Here's the short answer. If the person passes the following test, he is most likely an employee and therefore subject to withholding taxes:

- He works on your premises.
- You provide him with nearly all of the necessary equipment, tools, supplies, and resources necessary to perform his work.
- He does not perform similar work for other companies while working for you.

For example, John is a computer repair technician. He comes to your shop on call. If he is able, he fixes your computers on the spot, using his own tools. If not, he takes them back to his home-based basement workshop and repairs them. John has six companies just like yours under contract to provide such services. Upon completion of the job or on a monthly basis, John sends you his bill and you pay it. John meets the test of an independent contractor.

On the other hand, Roberto, a real estate agent, works out of your office full time. He does not pay any portion of your rent. You provide him with a desk and telephone and use of the copier, fax machine, and computers. You provide him with the shared services of an administrative support staff person. Even though he purchases his direct-mail postcards from your franchisor, pays his own cell phone bill, and uses his personal car to list and show homes, Roberto qualifies as an employee.

A real estate associate was accused of leaving a door open during a cold snap while showing a home. The heating pipes burst and flooded the house. The owners of the real estate agency tried to claim that the associate was an independent contractor and therefore not covered by their insurance. They tried to force him to personally pay for the damages. Based on the IRS definition of an independent contractor, the judge in the case ruled that the associate qualified as an employee and therefore his actions were covered by the agency's insurance policy.

You Are Only as Successful as Your Team

No matter how well-intentioned or talented you are, you will be much better with experienced outside experts helping you. You simply can't know everything yourself. There are many highly qualified accountants, marketers, public relations experts, web developers, and tax attorneys practicing in smaller firms and even as sole practitioners. Find the right ones for you. In a start-up, size, pricing, and fit with your entrepreneurial pace are critical. We made the mistake many years ago of hiring an accounting firm that was too large for us. While they may have meant well, we simply could not afford their rates as a small start-up. Every time we asked the manager what the firm's services would cost, he would say, "Don't worry about it." When the bill finally came, we had to work out a protracted payment plan. Ask and get answers up front to the following questions:

- How long has the firm or individual been in business?
- Do they work with start-ups, and do they have special terms for them? (Some very large firms have special "startup" service groups within them.)
- Who will actually service your account and what is that person's level of expertise?

- What does the firm charge and what services do they feel you will need?
- What professional designations do the staff members or partners have and how much continuing education do they receive?
- What experience do they have with companies in your industry?
- Do they handle any of your direct competitors and do they have a policy of not handling competing clients?
- Are they prominent in their field? Do they speak at conferences? Have they been featured in the press or interviewed in the media?
- Can they demonstrate helpful insight and guidance beyond crunching the numbers?
- Are they well networked and able to refer you to other people that can help you grow your business?

Many years ago, Barry's ad agency, a market research firm, a law firm, and an accounting firm all helped a client write the business plan that won him the investment he needed to launch his new, expanded operation. In appreciation, the client invited all of us out to dinner at a fancy restaurant. Midway through dinner, the accountant leaned over to my wife and me, indicating that there was only one reason why the operation would fail, as he pointed to the client. Within three months, the client had failed to pay nearly everyone in town. From that moment, I hired that accountant and kept him as my business and personal tax advisor for seventeen years. Look for wisdom, as well as professional expertise.

Straight Talk about Taxes for Start-Ups

Are there legitimate ways the small business start-up can reduce its tax liability? According to Salim Omar, yes. Pay careful attention to his advice.

Critical to start-ups and taxes, Omar echoes our advice above: "Pay them when they're due; the IRS and the state are the last places you want to borrow from." Don't bring in employees unless you can pay their payroll taxes. Employee leasing may be advisable, since the employee leasing company is responsible for paying the taxes. Hiring a payroll company can assure you meet the payroll tax deadlines. Managers can now be held liable for payment of taxes even if they don't own the business. The government is your first creditor.

As we previously stated, Omar concurs structure is critical when it comes to taxation. Today, there are fewer reasons for start-ups to become an S or C corporation. Previously, there was an advantage in deducting health insurance premiums. That advantage no longer exists. However, Omar advises, if you're planning to do an IPO (Initial Public Offering), you should probably organize your business as a C corporation. Why? It will be easier to sell the shares when you become publicly traded. You can still start as an LLC and then change to a C corporation, depending on the owner's growth plans and exit strategy.

Reducing and Mitigating Tax Liability

If you have organized your business as a sole proprietorship, a partnership, or an LLC, you may pay less in taxes if the net income is over $94,000. You will experience a savings by not paying self-employment tax. If your business has a net income of under $94,000, an S corporation may mean lower taxes for you. Omar advises you review the legal structure of your business annually to determine whether or not to change it. S and C corporations are essentially taxed doubly—on both the income of the entity and that of the owner operators.

Hiring your children to work in your business and putting them on the payroll can reduce your taxes by shifting the tax liability from a highly paid employee (presumably yourself) to a lower-paid employee (your child). Omar recommends you then set up a Roth IRA to grow that child's earnings, tax deferred.

Do not miss out on the home office deduction. It is no longer necessary that your home be your principal place of business if you use a home office for administrative or management activities not performed elsewhere. You may deduct a proportionate share of the square footage of your home's expenses for the room you use as a home office—mortgage, utilities, property taxes, etc.

Good record keeping is essential to claiming your entitlement to all of your deductible expenses. Next to undercapitalization, poor record keeping ranks at the top of the list for why small business start-ups fail. You must keep track of everything—miles driven, ordinary and necessary business expenses. Omar reminds us that you should try to tie things to the business. For example, can you deduct the expenses from a trip you took that included both vacation and business? Yes, provided you performed business activity in your line of work or you attended a convention. However, he quickly adds, you are unable to write off six days of vacation if you only spent one day of the week away at the convention. Further, your spouse's airfare is not deductible if she does not work in the business.

Retirement plans are an excellent way of mitigating the tax liability for your start-up. If your business is profitable, start a small business retirement plan. Start with a traditional IRA or a Roth IRA. Later, you can change to a SEP, where the contribution limits are higher, or a 401K. The money saved will grow tax deferred. The business will not pay the tax; the individual will pay it later.

Rent out either your personal residence or your vacation home to your business. This little-known strategy could keep money in your pocket. The business can pay the rent and deduct the rent. You can use it for boards of directors, shareholder, or staff meetings. The income received by the business owner is not taxed. You are permitted to do this for up to fourteen days per year.

People who own a rental property can defer the capital gain from the sale of that property to a 1031 Exchange if they purchase another property. However, it must be done through an intermediary. When they sell the second property, they can place part of the capital gains into another 1031 Exchange and continue to defer the tax. Omar advises that you can do this indefinitely.

What impact can these practices have on your small business start-up? According to Omar, "Through tax planning, saving, and retirement planning, the start-up can amass a huge amount of money. For example, just $4,000 invested annually for forty years at an average return of 9 percent will yield a return of over $5 million."

How to Save Big on Administrative Costs

The list of things you have to be aware of can be more than a little daunting, especially to someone in a start-up. Keeping all of the personnel and staff administration issues straight can get in the way of your core business, distract you from what you really want to be doing, and potentially put your entire business at risk if you make a mistake. Even more importantly, you need to focus your time on activities that will turn a profit for your enterprise. The management of people in this post-Enron era has become a full-time job, and unfortunately, the same requirements often apply whether you are a company of five or 500. One way to avoid these complications and lower your risk and often your administrative costs, is to outsource the complete human resource management function to people who do it full time. Outsourcing this function saves you money, plain and simple. One of the great advantages of doing business in the 2000s is that because of the complexity and risk involved in many aspects of business, specialized companies have been created to take over these tasks for you.

A great example of this is a company like Administaff. With Administaff, you and all your employees become employees of Administaff, where you can benefit from existing and highly refined people management systems. All of the tasks that can be so time consuming, like payroll management, taxation, legal compliance, and training of management and employees concerning workforce issues, can all be done by the highly trained Administaff managers. And with an outsourced personnel firm like Administaff you get the expertise of a personnel system that manages hundreds of thousands of employees, gaining you group pricing on things like insurance and employee benefits, saving you still more money.

To gain these benefits, you do pay a relatively small fee to Administaff or one of its competitors, but typically much less than you would if you hired a full- or even part-time human resource manager. While you may want to bring these functions in-house as you grow, the advantages of using an outsourced human resource management firm are immense when you are starting up because:

It's faster. Especially when you're starting out, you can reduce the time involved in dealing with personnel issues by orders of magnitude.

It's systematic and complete. What is amazing to the nonprofessional is how complex human resource issues have become. One meeting with a professional outsource group will likely convince you that this is, as they say on TV, something you shouldn't try by yourself at home. Companies like Administaff have spent years developing and refining systems that would be difficult, time-consuming, and expensive to recreate.

It's less risky. Two great advantages of technically making your employees someone else's employees by using a staffing company are that you have a buffer against legal and financial repercussions and a trained management staff to handle employee complaints, sexual harassment issues, and management-employee confrontations. These outsourced firms can train you on all management/legal issues and help you train your employees and managers as well. If problems do occur, they can intervene in a professional way that does not drain your personal attention or time.

It lets you focus on your core business. This is perhaps the most important benefit of human resource outsourcing. No entrepreneur has the time to focus on the business of building a business as well as the business of human resource management. Look at the issues and costs, but outsourcing these services will certainly make sense for most start-ups much of the time.

Outsourcing Warehousing, Shipping, and Inventory

Another way to accelerate the development of your business is to use specialized outsourcing services for your warehousing, shipping, and inventory management. What many entrepreneurs don't realize is that some of the most expensive and difficult aspects of logistics management can now be outsourced on a purely variable cost basis. Instead of having to make significant investments in warehousing space and shipping trucks, you can do what companies like Amazon and Dell did as innovators in their respective market areas. In fact, it is not too much of an overstatement to say that Amazon's business was almost entirely built on the new technologies that allow a company to build a virtual infrastructure.

Think about it. Amazon owned no inventory, no ware-houses, no trucks, hired no delivery or warehouse personnel, yet was able to become, almost overnight, the world's largest book-store. Taking advantage of the Internet as a virtual store, Amazon was able to use the inventory and warehouses of America's publishers and shipping services like FedEx to overcome barriers to entry that had protected large publishers for years. You can do the same.

Dell Computers is another example of a major company that built its business by assembling pieces of systems and inventory from specialized partners so that it could focus on attracting customers and meeting their needs for customized computers. Unlike its competitors Hewlett Packard, Compaq, and IBM, Dell spent no money on building warehouses or stocking inventory that might or might not sell as predicted. Instead, Dell used a logistics plan built for it by Eagle Global Systems and the eighty warehouses that Eagle owns to store the components for its machines in geographically efficient markets. The money that Dell saves using virtual warehouses and having inventory available on a just-in-time basis allowed it to lower its prices and create a market position that allowed it to beat its older and more established competitors in ways that previously couldn't be imagined. Again, you can do the same.

SMART-START TIP

Outsource!

Unless your start-up business is human resources, staffing, shipping, inventory management, or warehousing, there is usually a tremendous advantage to outsourcing these activities. You'll save investment money, be more efficient, benefit from other people's expertise, and be able to focus on your core business.

Insurance You Absolutely Need

One of the unfortunate aspects of being a start-up executive in the current business climate is that we are all much more liable to legal consequences, not only of what we do, but what our employees and officers and directors may do. Fortunately, there is insurance to protect you against almost all occurrences. This doesn't mean you shouldn't do everything you can to protect against wrongdoing, but you really need to understand the risks that are out there and look at the best possible insurance you can acquire.

Fidelity and Crime Coverage
According to AIG Insurance, the average American business loses 6 percent of its annual revenues to employee theft. This is a high cost for any company, but since this kind of theft occurs much more often in small- to mid-size firms, it can be particularly devastating to a start-up. Additionally, the forms of employee theft often occur over a long term, and when those losses are discovered the impact can be devastating. There are insurance products that cover things like employee theft of money and securities, forgery, robbery, computer funds transfers, and Internet media issues.

Directors and Officers Insurance (D&O)
The only way you will be likely to attract the quality officers and directors who you will want to help you in your business is to protect them personally and professionally from undue risk from being associated with your company. Make sure that if your firm is sued—and it can be sued for all kinds of reasons, some of which may be frivolous—the legal issues and risks for your directors and officers are minimized. The key to that is Directors and Officers Insurance, an absolute must-have. In addition to protecting your directors and officers, you will be

protecting yourself as the key officer and director from personal and professional risk.

While many executives of privately owned companies feel that their largest risk is exposure to litigation from employment violations—and that surely is an area of concern—according to Monitor Liability Managers, LLC, litigation against directors and officers can be even more devastating and prevalent. According to Monitor, "The insured that are experiencing these claims are located all over the United States and operate in many different industries." Things that directors and officers have to be concerned about include antitrust violations, securities violations, unjust compensation, fraud, and misrepresentation, among others.

Let's say that you and your fellow officers and directors do everything possible to create policies that are above board and do everything in your power to run a great company, as we know you will. What's troubling is that things your employees do, even without your awareness, can put the company at risk for litigation—litigation that could put your company out of business. Monitor, for example, describes a case in which they are defending a company for the actions of two of their salespeople, who are being accused of using confidential information and databases from a previous employer to gain competitive advantage. A firm like Monitor, because it provides the insurance, fights for its insured, and having a fine insurer can be one key to getting sleep at night for any start-up entrepreneur.

Errors and Omissions (E and O) Insurance

Firms and individuals rendering professional services like attorneys, accountants, engineers, and surveyors are constantly at risk of being charged with having committed a material error or omission (i.e., a mistake) by their clients. According to Joseph Rybarski, president and CEO of Financial Specialty Risk Management, a national firm specializing in management risk insurance, "Even though the charges are frequently overblown or just plain false, there is a significant expense in defending against these claims."

Insurance covering such defense costs along with potential adverse judgments is a solution to insulate you from a career-threatening catastrophe. Aside from the insurance component itself, you will have immediate access to experienced attorneys who will provide you with immediate help when charged with a negligent act. This alone often eliminates or mitigates a claim before it gets out of control.

While many professionals are required by law to have some level of professional liability (E&O) coverage, it just makes sense to protect your livelihood even if you're not being forced to do so.

Smart-Start Summary: Keys for Managing Your Human Capital and Saving Big on Administrative Costs

1. The minute you hire employees, you need professional HR advice.
2. Have clearly articulated workplace policies that will pass legal tests.
3. Invest in training; productivity spells profitability.
4. We live, work, and conduct business in a litigious society.
5. Protect yourself with outsourced HR.
6. Control your costs with outsourced payroll, staffing, and warehousing services.
7. Insurance pays more than it costs and it lets you protect the long-term value of your start-up.

9

Execute a Winning Growth Strategy

Decide from the outset what you want your business to look like—both now and later. It's not just about structure. What size business can you manage? How wide do you want to reach? How many clients can you service adequately? How global do you want to become? How long do you plan to operate it? How many employees can you manage? How many revenue streams can you implement, generate, maintain, and grow?

When you answer all of these questions, you can truly design your business and its outcomes. Don't wait for it to take shape. Shape it the way you want it from the outset. It all starts with you. Lead, don't follow. Lead in your organization; lead in your industry; lead in your community. How do you do this?

Lead Through Innovation

Innovate, first and foremost. Innovate new products; innovate new services; innovate new delivery systems; innovate new distribution channels; innovate new employee acquisition and retention models; innovate new customer care and retention programs; innovate new marketing opportunities. You don't have to be an innovator in every way—but being a leader in at least one area gives you a great Start-Smart advantage.

Study the companies that develop a culture of openness and innovation. Now, compare them to the companies that only grew through acquisition, or even worse, rest on their laurels. The innovators develop the habits, the flexibility, the culture—the very DNA of success. Companies that simply buy up other companies or accept past success as a predictor of future success, do not. They may remain stable players, for a while, but the pace of change is a part of our business landscape, and that stability can't last forever. As a start-up, you need the innovation mindset to always grow to the next level. Let's examine some real-world examples.

Take two small advertising agencies, each with a sole owner. Each owner operates his shop on a day-to-day basis, hands on. Each originated as a start-up with the owner at the helm of his ship. Both individuals worked for other people in their chosen field for many years before starting their own enterprises. Both men grew their businesses to a point where they derived a comfortable income for themselves. Both men generated enough business to hire staffs with several employees. Both men reached a level of success that allowed them to buy their own buildings.

Everything looks about equal so far, right? The similarity ends here. The first man built his personal wealth by producing high-quality brochures and printed collateral material for large pharmaceutical and health care companies. After many years of doing just that the landscape changed. His clients began to pull the design work in-house and began to send the printing overseas, mostly to China, all in an effort to save money. Market pressures forced them to return more to the shareholders on their investments. Efficiencies and economies dictated these moves. Unfortunately, our friend didn't see the changes coming. Worse yet, he did not react in time. He failed to redirect his efforts into another sector, to offer new and innovative services, or to prospect a different profile of client that would still want these services at his prices. The result? He had to layoff his entire staff, sell his building, and go back to work for someone else. The good news? It's preventable.

Let's look more closely at the second man. At almost exactly the same time as the above scenario, the second ad agency owner studied the marketplace, noticed that the printing industry in the United States had shrunk in size, and responded to the market with an innovation. Harvey Hirsch received a patent on a nontraditional process that involved die-cutting then printing, instead of the usual procedure. This resulted in the production of short-run, personalized, three-dimensional marketing and promotional pieces. Hirsch developed an entire product line that is changing the paradigm of direct-mail marketing. Instead of sending out a huge press run and hoping for a 1 percent response, Hirsch's clients send very few pieces targeted to only the most productive prospects (see *www.popandfoldpapers.com* and *www.DigitalDimensions3.com*). After a few refinements, a slew of graphic art industry awards, several very impressive client success stories with extremely high rates of return, he has now begun to franchise his operation and license out his technology. Innovation spells growth, period.

Look at the new generation of solid companies that began as start-ups in recent business history. Take Dell, Apple, Jet Blue, Starbucks, Amazon, FedEx: What common thread runs through all of them? They lead. And they lead the marketplace through innovation. Plain and simple, there is no room in today's competitive environment for me-too companies. Don't bother expending the huge effort to launch a start-up unless you have something new or better to offer the world. They don't need you. Rest assured, the market will tell you. If you don't wow them with something they absolutely crave, a competitor will bury you. So, what do people crave?

Well, we've already told you how to put your finger on the pulse of the market by doing research before you launch your start-up. It doesn't stop there. It has to continue through the life of your enterprise. So, what is "it"?

The Big "It"

It's all about the experience you provide. People today buy experiences, not just products and services. If a company designs its processes and procedures right, hires and trains its people right, creates and markets its products and services right, holds its customers' hands throughout their engagement, it will succeed, even if its " core product" is a commodity. When our clients in the travel industry offer trips, a commodity, they take pains to assure that the customer experience will go smoothly—and enjoyably—throughout the process. They sell an experience. Every contact your customers have, from the time they hear about you in a news story or an advertisement to the first call they make or first visit to your website to the ordering of your product or service to the delivery of the product or service to the packaging to the instructions to the first usage to the follow-up quality assurance call your staff makes, should create an unforgettable experience. People like to do business with people they like—make sure the experience you provide builds on that simple premise.

This is the stuff that supports a business's growth. Leave it out of the equation and you risk becoming an undifferentiated commodity. People don't engage with commodities. They seldom buy them again. They just look for the next bargain and buy someone else's brand. Not so with experiences. Create a phenomenal experience, and they will come back, they will tell everyone they know, " viral marketing" and your business will keep growing.

To get another perspective we talked to Kaushal Majmudar, who consults with many successful entrepreneurs and who earned his undergraduate degree from Columbia University and a law degree from Harvard University with honors. Majmudar has some important views on growth: "Get partners. Let one of you concentrate on operating the business while the other works on growing it."

According to Majmudar, who is a success in his own right, "Competition is an illusion. There is so much opportunity to delight customers, rather than putting energy into getting market share." He defines greatness as "the sum of a lot of little things done well." He praises the start-up: "Small businesses can innovate right away. Try things and integrate them into practice." At the same time he cautions, "Any one innovation has a finite life. "Instead, he advises, "Constantly think of a series of incremental innovations." He cites the Apple iPod, which sounds better, manages the process of acquiring and archiving music better, and has a better user interface, as well as the capacity to warehouse the user's whole music collection. He says of Apple's Steven Jobs, "He has an eye for detail . . . and he has a high standard—always wanting to make something better."

"Just responsiveness and reachability can be innovative." Majmudar further cites the extra care that so few businesses take to recognize their visitors by name on a reader board in the lobby. He offers this advice to small business start-ups looking for ways to innovate: "Any innovations that help people solve time problems or cut through the clutter of information to simplify our lives are good; anything to make things more convenient or more pleasing to interface with."

What do the winners do, according to Majmudar? They look at their businesses from the customers', employees', and suppliers' points of view. They engage in critical thinking. He advises entrepreneurs to, "Question their own assumptions and see if they hold up. Make the implicit explicit. Look at the value chain of the industry. See the gaps in what people are assuming. Ask how you can drive more value to the business. Can you drive down the cost and pass it on to the customer? Wal-Mart did this. Nobody said they had to."

How else can you enhance your growth strategy? Majmudar advises: "Have people that inspire and support you; read and learn from the masters; feed your mind. Figure out what you do well and find partners that do the other things you need done well. Outsource as much as you can. Create a business model with recurring revenue and performance-based compensation." Incentivize your customers for helping you acquire more customers.

Never stop planning. Keep a vision of where the business will be in five years, ten years, etc., in front of you. Begin with the end in mind. Passion leads to commitment, which leads to persistence, which leads to solutions, which leads to innovation, which attracts growth.

Smart-Start Approach to Growth: Planning—not Plans.

Most people spend more time planning a vacation in intimate detail than they spend planning their business. How can you arrive at a destination without a roadmap? But there is a major difference between a plan which is a static object, and planning which is an on-going and adaptive process. Plans will inevitably change, but your ability to plan and adapt will be a key to success. Mark Green is the CEO of Performance Dynamics Group, LLC (*www.time-for-change.biz*) and a business improvement specialist. He cites the importance of the strategic planning piece to the growth of a start-up right from the start.

"People launch into a business trying to be too many things to too many people. Their thought process is to cast a wider net; they have a fear of declaring too sharp a focus, of missing opportunities. Then you wake up one morning and realize, or an advisor helps you realize, that the reality is that you're not much to anybody. That hurts. You're running all over the place, but you're not able to build depth or build a team; you're spending too much time being busy. The path to more is to focus on less. You need to go through a process to determine what is really important to you and to understand why it matters. Put some stakes in the ground and declare a sharp focus for your business. It becomes easier to focus your limited resources on making that happen and to ask for the help of others to make that happen (through networking, etc.)."

Many people don't have a specific enough direction for where they are heading with their business. Mark makes this analogy: When he asks a client what direction they are going with their business he often gets answers that equates to, "I'm heading West," as opposed to, "I'm heading for a meeting at the Golden Gate Bridge, the South Tower, at 2:30 P.M." "There is a real need for entrepreneurs to go through a process to help them understand what they really need, why that matters, declare a specific focus for their business, and then build an actionable plan to get there and use that to help them enlist others to help them get there."

The Process

When you follow a process, you get more predictable results. You should use a process for planning your business. Picture an upside-down triangle. Start with broad thinking, questioning, and concepts. Narrow step by step: Above the top of the triangle is strategic thinking; at the bottom of the triangle is a tactical plan.

The strategic thinking element has four steps: development of vision, development of core values, an external assessment, and an internal assessment.

Development of Vision

This is a broad statement of what you want to accomplish in the long term. When it's done properly, you can use it as a filter to make decisions, and your employees can use it to drive their behavior. It's not a marketing statement; many companies confuse these things. It should be short, and capture the real inspiration of the business. In the best visions, there is an aspect of nobility and something that can inspire a team to do great things. The vision statement is critical because it forces you to focus, it differentiates your company, and can be something that motivates your employees and clarifies how they should act. Let's look at an example of a vision statement that works and which has driven one of America's most successful companies, Wal-Mart. Early on, here's what Sam Walton said: "If we work together, we'll lower the cost of living for everyone . . . we'll give the world an opportunity to see what it's like to save and have a better life." It's not about cheap products, it's about a much bigger vision, letting the world have a better life. And that vision, so big, so broad, has inspired growth that has been unrivaled in the retail channel.

Development of Core Values

These are the non-negotiable rules that govern behavior in your organization. There should be only four to six, and they should be behaviorally defined. Let's take Mark Green's core values as an example: "To always question the status quo." Your core values will determine how you behave and accomplish your goals.

In Green's example, he explains: "We won't enter into a relationship with anyone if we are more committed to their success than they are." If somebody violates one of your core values, it is serious enough to call for their removal. Vision and values together start to define how you are going to behave as an organization and what you are shooting for. You cannot over-communicate them. For example, at Wal-Mart, during shift changes employees recite their creed before they come face to face with customers. It works.

An External Assessment

Look outside at the environment around your business: competition, competitive advantages and disadvantage, industry trends, customer trends, and government regulations. Look at everything that has the potential to impact the business.

Internal Assessment

Look inside. Whether you have one or 1,000 employees, you use the same process. Ask: How is our organization structured? How do we communicate internally? What are we really good at? What are we not good at? Also, what are our SWOTs?

SWOT-Strengths, Weaknesses, Opportunities, and Threats

As you do your planning, it is important to recognize that no matter how great your concept is, your team is, or your marketing is, there are in every organization weaknesses as well. For every major opportunity you see, there are threats that can jeopardize your business success. It may be easier to see and talk about your Strengths and Opportunities, but you will do well to spend as much time analyzing your Weaknesses and Threats. Because once you identify them, you can take action to address them.

From the internal and external analyses, we can then come to some conclusions about opportunities, risks, and threats. Take those and categorize them according to their potential impact on your business as well as short or long term. Make quadrants—high impact/short term, etc. Look at them through a lens of prioritization. This last step in the strategic thinking piece of the process often changes the priority. That is the value of the process. High-impact, short-term items should receive first priority.

Now, start the tactical planning process. First, determine your business-plan objective (others call it a mission statement). This should be a definitive, measurable statement at the highest level of what you are going to accomplish in the next period (usually twelve to eighteen months).

Next, create critical success factors (CSF). These are categories or areas in the business that must be addressed in order to achieve the business plan objective. There should be between four and six of them. They could be staffing, marketing, sales, or individual development. Develop your goals for each of your CSFs. They become the stepping stones to achieving your business-plan objectives.

Next, create a dashboard for your business. Green advises you select three to four indicators that you need to track and monitor through the year to make sure you are on track. Most start-up entrepreneurs shy away from this process thinking planning will become cumbersome and onerous. It should not. The initial planning process should take from twelve to eighteen hours. If you break it down, you can accomplish it over a period of weeks, devoting just one to two hours per week. But then, make sure the ongoing review and adjustment of the plan, "the planning" becomes an ongoing part of your business management system. Remember Green's advice: "Are you too small to have a plan or are you thinking too small not to have a plan?"

How will your garden grow?

Smart-Start Summary: *Tools to Develop Winning Growth Strategies*

1. Consider hiring a qualified business coach to map out a growth strategy.
2. Your business growth plan is as important as your business launch plan.
3. Lead through innovation.
4. Provide a superior customer experience.
5. Make planning an ongoing part of your business system.

10

Build on Other People's Success: Franchises, Partnerships, and Purchases

One of the things that many first-time entrepreneurs forget is that you don't always have to go it alone. Depending on the type of business you are interested in, there are a variety of ways in which you can enhance your chances for success, minimize your risks, and reduce your stress. One of the great things about American business in this new century is that everywhere you go there are new opportunities to partner with other businesses for mutual benefit. In the past, collaboration may have been seen as a weakness—the thought being, "If I'm so good, I should be able to do this all myself." Now, even the largest firms—think Dell—use partnerships to accelerate their growth, reduce their risks, and maximize returns.

For a start-up executive, there has never been a better time to build your business by building on the successes of companies who have done all or part of what you have conceived in your business plan. It is extremely comforting to know that in almost every aspect of your business someone has preceded you, taken the initial risks, made the inevitable first mistakes, and somehow survived so that you can benefit from their pioneering efforts.

There are four major ways you can use the successes of others to ensure your own success. At least one of these approaches, and maybe all of them, can be combined at various times of your businesses's life to accelerate your growth and enhance your success. The four approaches you should consider are:

1. Franchising as a franchisee
2. Franchising as a franchisor
3. Strategic partnerships
4. Buying an existing business

Becoming a Franchisee

Franchising is an attractive approach for many people who want to start their own businesses. The proof of that is that according to a study by Pricewaterhousecoopers, one of every twelve businesses in America is a franchise. And the pace of franchise openings is not slowing down; in fact, according to this same study, there is a new franchise opening in this country every eight minutes.

To gain key insights into the benefits and risks of franchising, we worked with Wayne Bunch JD, LLM of Jackson Walker LLP, *www.jw.com*, an expert on the franchise industry. Bunch is uniquely qualified to talk about succeeding through franchising because he is that rare individual who combines technical knowledge with personal in-the-trenches experience. Bunch is an entrepreneur who has built several successful businesses, a franchisor who built and sold a franchise company with more than one hundred units nationwide, and a legal expert and theorist who advises other companies in the franchising world. So his perspective encompasses both the specialized day-to-day issues of making payroll and the larger regulatory and systematic issues that are keenly important.

In addition, Bunch speaks with that true sign of someone who should be listened to: he begins by telling you about his mistakes. The first thing he will tell you when you sit down with him is, "I identify with people in franchising because I know the fears and worries that surround any new venture. The goal in a start-up is not to avoid mistakes; you can't. It is to survive them." And this from a man whose franchise, Crescent City Restaurants, won the 2004 Nation's Restaurants Magazine Award as Hot Concept of the Year.

As Bunch says, "The reason why becoming a franchisee makes sense for many people is that someone else made most of the mistakes. By the time a franchise is made available for license by franchisees, it should have already overcome all of the typical start-up errors and have created a replicable model of a successful business." Finding the right franchise partner can be a way to making your start-up truly successful.

A successful franchise operator is a business partner who will provide you with much of what you need for start-up success:

- A tested business plan that you can use to raise capital
- Operational systems that have been tested and proven successful
- Products that have been shown to have a large consumer audience
- Marketing and sales models plus a national brand and ad campaign
- Buying power and economies of scale for lower prices
- Legal and regulatory systems
- Training programs that show you how to start up your business and train your employees

One can see from this list that what the franchisor provides looks promising as a way of increasing your chances of success.

But what are the issues that get in the way of franchise success—because even franchisees fail. The most important issues are choosing the right franchisor and being appropriately capitalized. "Entering a franchise relationship is like entering a marriage," says Bunch, "It's a long-term arrangement, typically ten years; it is literally for better or worse; money causes most of the problems, and you better find a partner in whom you can trust."

As a franchisee, three key steps in ensuring your success are:

1. **Finding the franchisor** that will help guarantee your success
2. **Finding the franchisor** that will act like a partner
3. **Finding the franchisor** that has built a successful and transferrable franchise model

After doing all the research necessary to find the right franchisor partner the franchisee's responsibilities are executing the franchise plan, managing the day-to-day operations according to the plan, and raising the capital to purchase the franchise and open the franchise operations. These are not trivial or unimportant responsibilities, but they will be immeasurably easier to achieve if you have chosen the right franchise partner from the beginning.

One last word from Bunch on why franchisees fail even if they have chosen the right franchisor partner: "When franchisees fail in a good franchise system, it is typically from two reasons: they don't have the requisite business experience to execute the business plan, or even more typically, they are undercapitalized."

Ways to assure the success of even a good franchise start-up:

Make sure you understand the business you are entering and have experience to run it.

Be sure you have enough capital to get through the first six to twelve months of the business start-up phase when it may be running at a negative cash-flow level. Bunch estimates that in a franchise that requires $300,000 to start, typically $100,000 will be needed from equity (your own personal investment), while $200,000 will typically be available to you as debt from Small Business Administration loans. This 70 percent to 30 percent debt-to-equity model seems standard, according to Bunch.

Work realistically with your franchisor to understand what that negative operating cash flow amount may be—too many franchisees enter the business thinking they can draw salaries from month one.

Work the franchise plan as it is delivered to you, it has worked elsewhere. That's why you are paying them a royalty and a start-up franchise fee.

Not every franchisee succeeds. Not every miner who went to California found gold. But following the success models of people who have already created successful replicable businesses may be the single best way to ensure your start-up if you are interested in competing in an industry that has a franchise model available.

Becoming a Franchisor

Perhaps you see yourself as the true entrepreneur, the pioneer who has the insight to build the next great business by himself. You can still benefit from the franchise concept by becoming a franchisor yourself. Here's where franchising can provide you access to what all businesses need to grow rapidly: OPM and OPP. To grow rapidly, almost every business needs access to OPM—Other Peoples' Money. In a world in which finding growth capital can be difficult or prohibitively expensive, raising money through franchising your concept can be the fastest and least expensive way to access OPM. By selling franchises you raise the money you need for rapid growth in the amounts you need without giving away equity or acquiring debt. In the franchisor model, your franchisees pay you money to buy into your concept and are also responsible for providing the capital to develop their individual franchises. This combination of investments from multiple franchisees can mean that in relatively short order you can access millions of dollars for growth capital, all coming from individuals who truly care about the success of your shared business.

In addition, the franchisor model allows you to diversify the business risk in rapid expansion by acquiring partners as franchisees who are highly motivated managers wanting to make your core business as successful as you do. One of the less talked about benefits of franchising is the acquisition of what we call OPP or Other Peoples' Passion. While access to growth capital is essential, the access to passionate managers who believe in your business model is something that is perhaps even more important and more difficult to achieve. When venture capitalists rate business plans, they often say the most important consideration is the management team. By this they don't just mean the skills these managers bring; what they are often looking for is the passionate commitment to success that is shared by multiple layers of management. A true partnership between franchisor and franchisees is one of the surest and quickest ways to find this level of truly passionate commitment to success.

Another benefit of franchising is rapid geographic expansion. If you believe your business can best grow through rapid geographic expansion in multiple locations, franchising can be the best solution to rapid growth.

All of the above assumes you are the successful pioneer who has built at least one successful business and that it meets the criteria for successful franchise development. But before we look at those criteria, let's look at the basics: What is a franchise and what do franchisors have to do?

What Do Franchisors Do?

According to Bunch, in its simplest form, "franchising is a systematic way of replicating a successful business model and of distributing products and services. It provides for aggressive growth while allocating risks and spreading the expansion costs."

As a franchisor you typically provide the franchisee with training and ongoing support for opening and operating a business that utilizes the franchisor's business systems and trademark(s) or service mark(s) (name[s] and logo[s]). A franchisee typically supplies the start-up capital and manages the day-to-day operation. The franchisee usually pays the franchisor an initial fee and ongoing royalties for the right to use the franchisor's marks and business systems and for ongoing support.

Under federal law franchising is defined as having three elements:

1. The franchisor has given the right to a franchisee to distribute goods and services under franchisors trademark, service mark, or other commercial symbol.
2. The franchisor has significant control or provides significant assistance to the franchisee. Examples include location approval, requirements of site design, training programs, operational manuals, and designated hours of operation.
3. Franchisee is required to pay at least $500 before or within six months of opening for business.

Assuming your business fits this definition, you must comply with the Federal Trade Commission Rule, which regulates the offering of a franchise business opportunity. Generally speaking, this rule requires that a prospective franchisee be provided with specific information about the franchisor, provided in a specific disclosure document called a Franchise Disclosure Document or FDD. This document will disclose all pertinent information regarding your company to a prospective franchisee and also includes all form franchise agreements used by the franchisor.

When and how prospective franchisees are disclosed with the FDD is also very well regulated by both the FTC and state regulatory bodies. For example, you must disclose a prospective franchisee at least fourteen calendar days prior to the signing of any franchise agreement or before the prospective franchisee pays any money to the franchisor.

Certain states have their own franchise regulations. In order to sell franchises in these states you not only have to comply with the federal guidelines, you also have to comply with the state guidelines. Most of these states require a registration process with state franchise agencies in order to sell franchises. A few of the more notable states where this is the case are California, New York, and Illinois. Texas law requires a one-time filing that costs $25.

Can You Be a Successful Franchisor?

According to a Pricewaterhousecooper study entitled "The Economic Impact of Franchised Businesses," franchising encompasses approximately seventy-five industries. One out of every twelve businesses is a franchised business. A new franchised business opens every eight minutes in the United States alone.

Just about any type of business can be franchised, whether selling products or services, from a storefront or from home, at retail or wholesale, or anything in between, but not every business meets the criteria for a successful franchise.

Here are some keys to consider if you dream about being a franchise creator yourself:

- ◆ **Concept**—You need a profitable business concept. Ideally, one that is unique, interesting, and has the potential for longevity.
- ◆ **Systems**—You must have developed systemized standards for operations. Your business systems are typically articulated in your operation manuals. It is important to note that your systems must be protected to the extent possible by claiming copyright protection, utilizing non-disclosure agreements and, as a practical matter, keeping your records private and out of the public domain.
- ◆ **Transferability**—The systemized standards of operation must be transferable. In other words, you must be able to teach the skills necessary to run the business profitably.
- ◆ **Prototype**—You must have a duplicable and profitable operating unit a franchisee can base her investment decision upon. Remember, it must be profitable enough that the franchisee can still make money after paying a royalty.

Operating a unit distinguishes you as a credible operator and one that has the ability to train and lead franchisees.

♦ **Brand Identity**—The business must have features and characteristics that distinguish it from the competition. This is done through trade dress, trademarks, and service marks. It is important to note that you must take the necessary action to protect these marks by registering them with the U.S. Patent and Trademark Office.

♦ **Team**—You must have a management team in place that can meet your company's obligations under the franchise agreement in support of its franchisees. This team must be capable of supporting franchisees in areas such as site selection, lease negotiations, prototypical plans and specifications, staff recruiting, staff training, marketing, product sourcing, customer service, etc.

Can You Attract Franchisees?

When thinking about your ability to use franchising as a successful growth strategy for your own business you need to think about numerous factors beyond the innate appropriateness of your business. First and foremost, to be a successful franchisor you have to get franchisees. This is similar to the concept of becoming a leader—first you have to get followers. No matter how attractive your business concept is, unless you have the marketing and sales skills necessary to recruit franchisees you won't be successful. Now think about this in terms of sports: Successful sports heroes often develop followers or fans. But there's more to it than just attracting potential fans, or franchisees.

To be successful as a franchisor you have to be a good developer of a duplicable business model and trainer in your system. Joe Montana was possibly the greatest quarterback ever to play the game, but his success was based on innate skills and abilities that he possessed, not necessarily on a system that he could teach or pass on.

On the other hand, Larry Bird, Kevin McHale, Robert Parish, Danny Ainge, and Dennis Johnson, all five starters on the championship winning Boston Celtics of the 1980s, have become successful coaches or executives who run and manage basketball teams. Whatever physical skills they had, they also inculcated a systematic approach to winning basketball games that could be passed on and replicated.

To be successful, a franchisor has to sell franchises and then the franchisees have to sell the products or services. The business, therefore, has to work on two levels. First, it must be attractive to prospective franchisees that are considering buying into a franchise system. And second, it must be profitable on the consumer level. Here's a summary checklist:

1. Do you have a prototype that can be replicated?
2. Is your prototype sufficiently profitable to provide your franchisee with an adequate return on their investment after paying royalties?
3. Will your concept work in other markets?
4. Will your product and services have longevity or is it just a fad?
5. Is the market for your product and services increasing?
6. Can you provide value to your franchisees after you have assisted them in opening and trained them in your systems?
7. Can your business be broken down into systems that can be easily taught and learned?
8. Have you considered who your target franchisees will be?
9. Does your business require an unusual skill set to be successful?
10. Will your present business survive if you devote substantial time and energy to starting a franchise company?

Forming Strategic Partnerships

You may be in the situation where franchising is not feasible or attractive to you. You can still benefit from OPP and OPS (Other People's Sales) through less formal means of partnerships. If there is one trend that is pervading American business, it is the idea that strategic partnerships are a key way to leverage growth, resources, and passionate commitment to business success. Every week we receive newsletters or invitations to industry groups explicitly designed to foster corporate networking with the goal of setting up strategic partnerships. This new trend is based on the following concepts:

Even the best companies can't be great at every aspect of the increasingly complex business competencies required to succeed in today's competitive environment.

There are new specialist firms whose entire business is to do exceedingly well a small part of your business. These might include advertising, selling, distributing, shipping, purchasing, even providing full- and part-time staff.

To focus on their core businesses means literally that— focusing. In order to provide all the products or services their customers may want; however, businesses can rent those services or products from partners who focus on other, complementary businesses.

Businesses can gain competitive advantage in being a full-service or full-product provider overnight not by building those services or products, but by private labeling products from other firms.

Partnering in co-marketing efforts with other firms lowers both firms' marketing spending while broadening market awareness and creating barriers to entry from competing firms.

Partnering allows businesses to accelerate their growth through access to new products, markets, or support systems.

Buying an Existing Business

You may have already decided that starting a business from the ground up would prove too overwhelming. Perhaps you haven't found a franchised business that interests you. Consider buying out an existing business, a going concern. But as always, we advise you not to try this at home, so to speak. Get help from the experts. Seek out a business broker—an intermediary with experience and a vested interest in bringing a qualified buyer and a qualified seller together. He gets paid to get the deal done. Working with a broker provides you with several advantages over approaching a business owner yourself. We interviewed two well-established brokers to get their advice.

View from the Trenches

Scott Stein, of Zermatt Associates (*www.zermattassociates.com*), comments on the advantages of buying an existing business.

"First and foremost, you have customers; the reason for being in business. Buy a business with repeat customers; as soon as you take over, you have customers and probably current income. It makes it easier to borrow; banks are favorable to it. Suppliers usually give you instant credit. Reputation and goodwill are established; the business is top of mind with customers. And, the referral network from an existing business is valuable for a consultant or a contractor. For example, accountants and attorneys often refer clients. It could take years to develop those referrals if you started from scratch.

With an existing business, you have a format, an accounting system, a fulfillment system, a known sales system. It saves time and money having those in place. An existing business has employees, as well. It reduces your risk. It's easier for the first-time entrepreneur to adapt."

Stein further advises: "Look at a franchise in the industry you intend to start a business in. See how it operates; how they set up the business and how they market it—even if you don't intend to buy the franchise. It encompasses all the business wisdom of people in that industry."

Now, let's focus on the advantages to using a business broker. According to Stein, because of the internet it's easier to look at businesses on your own, whether they are independent or franchises. However, many of the businesses listed for sale online are listings of brokers. Brokers offer free advice in many cases, listings at no charge, and they are often working on commission for the seller, like in real estate. Buyers' brokers exist for larger businesses. They are more common in specialized industries such as durable medical equipment sales. Certain industries, such as the trade show industry or the broadcast industry often have a professional intermediary, as they are highly specialized.

It is more common for an existing company to have a broker on retainer or working as a buyer's rep for them to seek out another business to acquire. You must know if the broker is working for the seller. In business brokering, there is no multiple listing service; whereas in real estate, brokers share information through a formalized cooperative system.

A broker may have listings you can't find on your own. A business is more specialized than a home—it's harder to categorize and has more complicating factors. Once you're looking at a business to buy, it becomes imperative that both sides have both an attorney and an accountant. First-time buyers often don't realize the complexity and enormity of the transaction. Often some seller financing is involved. The broker should list the business' volume, earnings, and asking price. When the seller is more reasonable about the valuation they are more likely to do a deal. The broker has an interest in doing the deal so he will work with both sides to qualify them. A broker can suggest what others in that business category have done. A brokered transaction will have better (reconstructed) financials. Keep in mind, however, that in many states no certification is required for brokers.

So, how do you select a business broker? Stein advises you check out the industry's professional association, IBBA—the International Business Brokers Association (*www.IBBA.org*). He further advises this route for businesses under $10 million. For larger acquisitions, he advises using a mergers and acquisitions firm. These are Main Street businesses. See if the broker has a CBI designation, indicating she is a certified business intermediary. IBBA has regional chapters in your area. Be sure to look specifically for small business credentials. Stein adds, "Get advice from people in small business, not corporate America. Spend time with them."

Finally, check out this article by Jim Dietz online, where he gives you "The Questions Business Brokers Hope You Will Never Ask": *www.franchisesforsalebyowner.com/BusinessBroker Questions.html*.

Ask a Small Business Broker

We asked Lou Iorio of Corporate Investment International (*www.corpinvest.net*), who has functioned as a broker for the last twenty years, to elaborate further on the subject of working with business brokers.

"The broker's role is to package the business and bring it to market. The buyer needs to do his due diligence. The buyer is making an assessment of risk. The broker should present the seller's case and be responsive to the buyer so the buyer can assess the risk. For example, in a service business the customer base is important; the buyer should look to see if it is too concentrated with one client. In most cases, the broker represents the seller. A good broker understands that the buyer and the seller must build rapport and trust. The broker is an intermediary. Some brokers do represent the buyer. Usually, this involves larger transactions; often, someone who has a very specific target. The buyer can use more than one broker."

Here are Iorio's suggestions on how to select a broker:

- Look for experience. How many years has the broker been in the business?
- Look for academic background in the financial field.
- What is the broker's level of visibility?
- Look to see if the broker has professional affiliations such as IBBA membership.
- Get to know the broker personally; spend time with him.
- Look at the broker's portfolio of business offerings; what businesses does he have?
- Look to see if the broker has a specialty or expertise in a specific industry.
- How much documentation does the broker give you upfront?

Look for full disclosure upfront. For example, a commercial baker looking to sell mentioned to a prospective buyer that they had been robbed three times; they had never informed the broker. Dig deep, and be careful.

In many cases, the sticking point between buyer and seller with an existing business revolves around the valuation— agreeing on what the business is worth. A broker plays a significant role in determining the valuation. Formal valuations can be purchased from a couple of thousand dollars on up; sellers will typically pay for them to support their asking price. Broker involvement can help assure the buyer of a more realistic selling price, since the broker is not emotionally attached to the business and wants to get the deal done. Finally, brokers help assure the confidentiality of the transaction. This becomes critical, especially with certain Main Street business categories. For example, if the operators working in a hairstyling salon get wind of the owner's intention to sell, they will often leave. Their clientele usually leave with them. The result: a huge devaluation of the business. Without the steady trade it's only worth the value of the lease and the (depreciated) fixtures and equipment.

Iorio stresses that the due diligence should start with the buyer herself. Is she prepared to be a business owner? Does she realize she may be the last paycheck to be cut? She must have the ability to bear the good and the bad times. Does she have the communications skills to deal with employees? Iorio suggests a visit to *www.energyleadership.com*, where you will find an assessment tool to create a baseline to determine where you are attitudinally. After all, a business owner is a leader. Along with the assessment it includes a review by a professional coach (offered by IPEC, a training school for business coaches). Perhaps most importantly, Iorio advises, the buyer should engage an attorney with experience in business sales and transactions.

There you have it: Reduce your risk by enlisting the aid of those who have reviewed the details of the business you might want to buy, and by carrying the ball when it already has momentum by buying a going concern.

Smart-Start Summary: *Keys to Alternate Routes for the Start-Up*

1. Consider buying a franchise to increase your chances of success, especially if you have never launched a business before.
2. Consider joining forces with a strategic partner to lower your costs and increase your market presence, especially if your funds are limited.
3. Consider buying an existing business with the aid of a broker, especially if you need a customer base right away.

Chapter

11

Ten Great Businesses You Can Start Right Now

The preceding chapters have described what you need to do to start a business, but what business should you start? How should you decide? Here are our five things to consider in choosing a business and our choices of ten of the most attractive new business categories in the coming years.

1. First and foremost, consider your own personal skill sets and passions. If you have unusual talents, skills, or relationships that can give you a competitive advantage in a business make sure you consider incorporating those skills in your new business. Also, whichever start-up you choose, you will be spending a huge amount of time at it and doing something you truly enjoy, or even better, are passionate about, will make a serious difference in your ability to stick through the difficult times to success.

2. Second, consider your available funding—capital-intensive businesses with a long timeframe to positive cash flow are more risky and more difficult to fund.

3. Third, consider the demographics of the population; picking expanding niche markets or targeting growing demographic groups are good ways to give yourself a competitive advantage.

4. Fourth, consider the economy at the time of your start-up and what implications it may have on your business choices. Even in recessions there are areas of opportunity, as you will see in our list of ten businesses you can start now.

5. Finally, consider the meteoric impact of new technologies on your potential customer base.

All of these factors will have a tremendous influence on your likelihood of success. An increasingly diverse ethnic population and a rapidly aging population spell the need for certain products and services to satisfy those trends. Add to that an economic downturn followed by a gradually rebounding economy and the need for certain businesses just flashes like a beacon. Filter those needs through the lens of hyperfast technological changes and the businesses you should consider starting become crystal clear. We'll give you our top ten picks and the why behind each of them.

New Media

While traditional media are not yet dead, many are in serious trouble. The entire media landscape has changed in the age of the Internet. Many traditional media giants like the *Rocky Mountain News* have closed. The largest radio conglomerates like Clear Channel and Cumulus are fighting off bankruptcy. Even the venerable *Boston Globe* was on the verge of shutting down without attaining union concessions.

As we stated in the advertising section of the chapter on marketing, the way people consume media has changed. The savvy media operators understand that old and new media coexist side by side. They also understand that we are approaching a new era—the era of the convergence of media platforms. What does this mean? It means that media companies are no longer in the radio business, the TV business, the cable business, the newspaper business, or the magazine business. They are in the business of providing on-demand unique, compelling, and original content across platforms. Today's consumer wants his information and entertainment on whatever device she uses, wherever she happens to be. Media companies that fail to provide that will be in serious difficulty.

Here are some additional reasons why new media is a rich area for start-up consideration:

Clear opportunities to move into a media vacuum. Traditional media is down—newspapers declaring bankruptcy, terrestrial radio revenue is down, major TV networks' revenue are down—but people are still looking to communicate, and the new media are growing as fast as older media are going down.

Models for start-up success. Twitter, Facebook, YouTube, and MySpace are examples of companies that started as avocations that grew into major businesses. You can build on your passions to build success.

Very low cost of entry. Distribution on the Internet means that there are no longer major barriers to starting new media companies. Blogs like the Drudge Report started with one person writing and have expanded into much more important businesses because of the way traditional media have piggybacked on them.

Explosive growth. Viral marketing, word of mouth, and referrals have all led to explosive growth for businesses in ways the founders often never imagined.

Chances to build on other new media in what looks like a nonstop evolution. For example, one of the start-ups Michael is now advising is a new media version of traditional radio, but modified by the flexibility of the Internet. Two experienced radio professionals have come together to build an Internet radio company that allows major corporations to build on their existing marketing and develop privately owned Internet radio networks to exclusively promote their own brands. Initial reaction to this next new thing from even traditional media like the *Washington Times* is extremely positive.

In this world content is king, and your particular expertise may be the key to a real business success. Finding new ways to communicate information can lead to profits faster than you imagine. For a last example, just look at "Early to Rise" newsletters, a business built by using electronic marketing to market electronic content.

Web 3.0: Social Networking; Next Stop, Global Village

We've already discussed how we're in the era of the convergence of media platforms, where today's consumer of media wants his content on demand, wherever he is, on whatever device he is using. We've also discussed the shifts in generational marketing to address an audience that wants to remain in control as consumers. Now, add to these trends a movement into an era where people choose the groups and communities they wish to align with and to communicate with. Enter the age of the phenomenon of social networking. It's no longer just a place where your kids post a MySpace page or a Facebook profile. What does it mean to your business?

At lightning speed, whole groups of people of untold size can make or break your business by marshalling public opinion through the power of social networks. Like it or not, we have arrived at this juncture. We spoke to Peter Shankman (*www .shankman.com*), author of *Can We Do That? Outrageous PR Stunts and Why Your Company Needs Them*, creator of *www .HelpAReporter.com*, a site where publicists can monitor and respond to the needs of writers, and one of the pre-eminent gurus of social networking.

According to Shankman, the biggest trend right now in social networking is a radical shift toward transparency. He says that companies are now realizing that a blog written by an intern for a CEO removes the trust level. Companies are becoming aware of the need to put out a high level of trust. As for future trends, Shankman sees a move toward one network.

"Everything we do is going to be on one network—a combination of our personal and our professional lives. It will give people more of a reason to love their job. Otherwise, it will be obvious; there has to be more than 'I went out to lunch.'"

So, is social networking here to stay or a passing fad? Shankman feels it will become part of the lexicon. Ten years ago, for example, looking up something on Google was brand new; now, it's part of the lexicon—people Google everything. Since the young people were the early adopters of social networking, one wonders, as baby boomers become users, will teenagers no longer see it as cool? Shankman thinks not: "Teenagers grow up. My parents are both NYU professors, and they're on Facebook."

Other social networks like LinkedIn and Plaxo launched to serve business people. So, how useful is social networking as a business tool? Are the social networks themselves profitable business models? We asked our expert.

"It's a tool that allows you to greatly expand on good customer service. If you do not have good customer service to begin with, it's not going to help you. Your job is to get other people to do PR for you. If you deliver stellar customer service, people will tell others about it." Just do your job well; have a great offline customer service program and armies of customers will spread the word for you across social networks where they communicate with their peers. Shankman believes the social networks will figure out how to make money in time.

If used improperly, can social networking backfire and hurt your business? Absolutely. Shankman relates how NASA lost credibility when they said they were tweeting from space and were not. Now, there are always people who can find you out. "The seventeen-year-old without a date one weekend will bring down your company—not the hacker from Russia."

A word of advice in the do's and don'ts area from our expert: "Be smart about what you're doing; it's mostly common sense. Don't jump on the latest whiz-bang technology . . . have a better reason—not because it looks cool."

Is this for you or does it only apply to certain types of businesses? According to Shankman, every business that's smart will figure out a way to use social networking, realizing that it will be in their best interest, sometimes, just to listen to what your audience is talking about and what they're doing. Also, to listen to your competitors—you can find out what people dislike about them that you can do better. He advises you see who the people online call experts and listen to those people.

Serving the Growing Aging Population

The second best-selling book in American history, (after the Bible) is Doctor Spock's guide to raising babies. Why? Because it was published when the first of the baby boom generation was born, and anxious parents bought it by the millions. The 76 million baby boomers have created business successes for the entrepreneurs who were clever enough to anticipate the next life-stage needs of this massive group. From Doctor Spock to Dick and Jane to Clearasil, Lipitor, and Viagra, products that were little used or unimportant became culturally dominant when the baby boom needed them. As the baby boom turns sixty, business opportunities will abound in this burgeoning aging population. Service this population and your business will flourish for years to come.

For example, retirement living communities, assisted living communities, and nursing and boarding homes will continue to open and prosper. In-home caregivers (skilled nurses, nurses' aides, and home health aides/homemakers), durable medical equipment, and medical supplies will satisfy an ongoing need. The obvious companion piece to these services: long-term care insurance. Think about the changing life-stage needs of a maturing population and opportunities will become clear. For example, when companies like Microsoft, Intel, and Philips—all high-tech powerhouses—start focusing business units on serving hospitals and in-home health care, you know the aging phenomenon is gaining real traction.

Think, too, about businesses that have traditionally been somewhat taboo in our culture—funeral services, casket sales, cremations, hospice, diabetes supply, even electronic mobility devices—and you will find not only traditional companies addressing these areas but new online approaches to meeting these needs. After all, when Costco started selling funeral caskets in their stores you have to believe there must be a real opportunity in this aging segment.

Automobile Service

As the U.S. auto industry finds itself in turmoil and new vehicles have become cost prohibitive for many, people are keeping their cars longer. This translates to a more frequent service cycle. In addition, today's autos require specialized training; fewer people have the know-how or the specialized equipment required to do their own repairs. Once again, the impact of technology, such as computer chips that control our cars' functions, rules, and creates business opportunity. Add to this equation the time poverty most people experience—especially during an economic downturn when they are working long hours and second jobs—and you will find them at the doorstep of your quick-lube or tune-up center. Unless you have already acquired both the mechanical and business skill sets for this industry, consider the many franchises that will give you the template for success.

But please understand opportunity is not only limited to people with sophisticated skills. One of our friends, for example, has seen the potential in selling used and recycled tires. One man's trash, after all, can be another man's treasure. People who have a very old but still running car that they just use for short trips around town, for example, just don't see the need to buy new tires that may be more expensive than their very used cars.

Alternative Energy

As the 19th Century French writer Victor Hugo said, "Nothing is more powerful than an idea whose time has come." The first Earth Day celebration occurred in 1970. Eco-consciousness did not immediately convert to broad, sweeping eco-policy changes. Everything goes in cycles. The political climate of recent years dictated a more laissez-faire economy. America in particular did not have a comprehensive energy policy, but times change, leaders change, and priorities change. And for now, whether you believe climate change is something we can affect or not, political incentives are now focusing on ways to conserve or save energy or to generate it through alternative means.

Once again, opportunity knocks. Businesses have discovered that building co-generation plants to produce their own energy has resulted in cost savings. For larger users of electricity such as commercial bakeries, glass manufacturers, and other high-heat applications, the payback on the equipment takes only a few years. The tax benefits offered make it even more attractive.

Take it one step further. Even homeowners have begun to explore wind, water, solar, and geothermal energy options. Demand grows for these services, and since somebody has to provide them it might as well be you. And in certain states there are tax incentives for things like solar heating for homes that will guarantee these approaches will be implemented.

And remember, when you think about alternative energy your business opportunities can be significant, even though the start-up costs are not major. For example, some of our friends have recently started businesses that are marketing deregulated electricity to homes and commercial institutions. They didn't spend any developmental money; they just entered into a royalty-based marketing agreement with an energy provider. Another group of friends are marketing special blinds to reduce heating costs in homes. Again, they didn't develop these products; they acquired regional marketing licenses that have allowed them to start their businesses knowing they have a product that really works and has great consumer value. They even created marketing firms to deliver chemical supplements that improve the cooling properties of air conditioners.

Financial Literacy and Advice

The recent economic meltdown and abuses of the financial system illustrate the need for those who possess wealth to have unbiased, trusted professionals to guide them in preserving that wealth. Growing distrust of large institutions such as banks, brokerages, and mortgage companies opens the door for more entrepreneurial boutique firms where clients will receive increased hands-on, high-touch attention. As we experience economic downturns, people need more financial education to cope. Sadly, this is seldom taught in schools. The population at large does not have a high degree of financial education. All age groups in the population desperately need to learn how to manage money, how to invest wisely, and how to manage their use of credit. Any business that can fulfill this need will flourish. Take, for example, a franchise headquartered in California, known as Online Trading Academy (*www.tradingacademy.com*). This company has set up franchises around the world to teach the science of trading stocks, bonds, currency, and other financial instruments to people from all walks of life, many of whom have little or no knowledge of the global economy. Many have successfully transitioned to earning their living as career traders.

Another model you may have seen on television involves firms like Vector Vest, InvestView, and InvesTools. These firms provide stock-selection software and classroom training courses on investing methodologies. There are other companies that provide information and different approaches to financial advisory services and you can participate in a variety of ways with them. As large firms like Bear Stearns and Lehman Brothers go out of business, the opportunity for new financial advisory services that put the consumer more in control can expect to grow.

Legal, Financial, and Consumer Services in Which You Can Remove the Middleman

Any system or approach that puts consumers more in control of either their financial or legal situations and lets them save money at the same time will certainly gain attention from a maturing baby boom population. After all, this is the group that has always wanted to be in control of their destinies. Remember, they grew up with "Have it your way" from Burger King as their basic marketing mantra. They are also great appreciators of value, and they remain the most educated generation in our history. When you combine all those factors you get the context for building new businesses that can succeed rapidly with this group.

One firm that might inspire you as you think about building your own company is LegalZoom.com. Co-founder Brian Liu and his partners understood early on that the Internet gave them a tool that allowed consumers to create simple legal documents on their own for a fraction of the cost of using a lawyer. You may have heard the LegalZoom ads on radio or TV, and their formula for providing control, convenience, great value, and speed has allowed them to build a business that attracts more than 800,000 unique visitors per month to their website.

Think of it; instead of going to a lawyer, taking days and thousands of dollars, you can use LegalZoom in the privacy of your home, and in minutes you can use their Internet forms to incorporate a business, form an LLC, or even create a will, all for a fraction of the cost of having a lawyer do it. As you think about your choice for starting a business it will pay off for you to remember the LegalZoom formula of Internet, convenience, control, value, and choice. And no matter what business you eventually choose to start, you should seriously consider using LegalZoom to incorporate it.

Fitness and Wellness

All you have to do to understand how powerful the changes in the way we age are is to think of what grandparents looked like in the books and magazines when you were growing up. The famous painting "Whistler's Mother" will do as an example. And then compare that image of the grey-haired older woman in a chair with images of current sixty-plusers like Diane Sawyer, Candice Bergen, Susan Sarandon, Lauren Hutton, or Tina Turner. Wow! And let's not forget that Sean Connery was named *People* magazine's Sexiest Man Alive when he was turning sixty.

We have new images of what age is, and of course our average longevity has increased dramatically, to almost seventy-eight years. But living longer without good health is a very bad trade-off. We don't want to be old and frail, we want to be older and healthy and vital. Any business that can help here will certainly gain the attention of a growing percentage of the population.

A proactive health model is the key here. As the traditional medical model, big pharmaceuticals, and managed care have fallen short of our expectations for producing wellness, current and future generations will seek out alternatives. Rather than reactive care designed to treat or cure sickness, the population will demand a shift to a wellness model, which will result in cost containment. This opens the door to numerous business opportunities that address the needs of all demographic groups within the population.

The epidemic of juvenile "diabesity"—obesity that often leads to diabetes—demands attention from physicians, dieticians, and physical trainers. Changing the sedentary habits of an entire generation raised on video games and television and the dietary habits of a fast-food generation will take the collective efforts of many skilled practitioners.

On the other side of the coin, people are not only living longer they are living better. Entrepreneur Stan Cohen (*www .chiforliving.com* and *www.maturitymatters.net*) travels to adult communities, assisted living facilities, and senior centers to teach and lead sessions in low-impact exercises to the aging population. Stan asserts that just because they are aging doesn't mean people have to lose their mobility, balance, and flexibility. He contends that his programs also help with relaxation and even concentration. Ultimately, this helps people live more independently.

Another great area of opportunity has to do with online advice and food and health supplements. A great company that we work with that you can look at for ideas or inspiration as you think about this area is Life Extension. They are pioneers in providing state-of-the-art information about the latest in medical research about living better and longer. They also provide a great line of health supplements that they sell on the Internet through affiliates.

One company that clearly believes we will be living much longer is LifeFitness, the makers of aerobic equipment for health clubs. Whenever you use any LifeFitness equipment like their elliptical stair steppers or stationary bikes you can check out the target heart rate you should hit for your cardio workouts at any age past twenty. You'll be glad to know there's a target cardio heart rate for folks who are eighty and ninety, even one hundred.

Home Repair and Maintenance

Increasingly, as time poverty takes over, busy working couples will perform fewer home repair and maintenance functions themselves. In better economic times the smarter contractors will redirect their efforts to home upgrades—remodeling, add-ons, etc. In recessions, you can build great businesses focusing on repairing and adding cost-saving features like solar heating. In addition, as the systems in homes become more complex and require more specialized training, tools, and equipment people will rely even more on contractors, as with automobile repair. Heating, ventilation, and air conditioning (HVAC), water softeners, and home appliances often have computerized controls now. The average homeowner simply cannot keep up with these innovations, but you can.

And don't ignore the chance to be opportunistic—one entrepreneur we know built a successful start-up after a hurricane damaged numerous fences in his town. Building on the customer relationships he developed by helping them with these necessary repairs, he built an ongoing business by hiring crews to do the ongoing landscaping work for these clients. Great customer service in one area not only led to more fence repair referrals but to ongoing work in other home maintenance areas.

Medical Innovations of all Kinds

The cost of medical care is a real issue, and there are both high-tech and high-touch solutions. Even elective and cosmetic medical care can provide business opportunities. New Jersey physician Dr. H. William Song used to make house calls. Today, his patients come to him for minimally invasive cosmetic procedures like laser hair removal, skin resurfacing, weight management, etc. Patients receive treatment from trained staff members, under physician supervision, without paying the cost-prohibitive prices of a plastic surgeon. In today's highly image-conscious world, maintaining one's best appearance goes far beyond vanity. It may make the difference between finding a job or a mate—or not.

Of course, starting a business here may require special knowledge—just check out the site at Pathway Genomics a pioneer in direct-to-consumer genetic testing. Here, for a relatively small fee, you can send in a sample of your DNA and have test results for your genetic predisposition for more than one hundred medical conditions.

But other businesses may be built on your ability to build or market simple products. You may not be the inventor, but you could be the person who sources innovative new medical products from other countries or states. Owning distribution for products you license is a great way to lower the risk of starting your business. Todd Smith of Inter-Continental Equipment, LLC, exports construction equipment. His wife, an operating room surgical nurse, gave him the inspiration for a new service. Todd began buying up medical supplies from distressed hospitals that closed down and sending them overseas to third-world countries for cents on the dollar. Bandages, syringes, and other supplies would have ended up in the dumpster; instead, Smith created a win-win situation—he turned a profit and the people in developing countries found an affordable source for critically needed medical supplies.

People's Passions, Avocations, and Loves

Many successful entrepreneurs have turned their hobbies or passions into profitable businesses. And as long as your passion taps into the passions of a significant and underserved group you can build a great business while doing what you love. Consider the number of people involved in activities like crafts or lovers of pets. The opportunities are huge to service their needs. That's exactly how the folks who started pet insurance began. They realized that there were millions of pet lovers who would want expensive medical treatment for their pets and that insurance was a real need for them.

Even art collectors and custom framers provide business opportunities. As inspiration for your own search for a business to start, take a look at *www.myartspace.com*, which provides a place for fine artists to connect with art collectors. A similar model is that being used by some of our friends, Katherine de Stefano, Storme Dahl, and Pat Cunningham who love the affluent Western lifestyle and are building a business by helping Western collectors more easily buy Western art and artifacts including spurs, buckles, and saddles all on the Internet. This may seem like a strange way to start a business, but when you realize that those buckles can cost $20,000 or more and saddles can go up to $120,000, you can see the power of building businesses around things both you and your customers love.

Appendix

A

Real-World
Start-Up Stories

Now that we have presented you with the advice of some of the most distinguished advisors to successful start-ups as well as the authors' own in-the-trenches insights on how to start, operate, and grow a business, we would like to offer you several firsthand accounts from recent entrepreneurs—folks like yourselves that grabbed their dreams by the horns and took the plunge into entrepreneurship. Each one tells their own recent start-up success story, which may inspire you or give you one important insight that will be applicable to your own business.

She Did It Her Way

Mary Repke, CEO of Coakley Business Class, LLC, a company that sells unique business luggage, carved out her own path to entrepreneurship with all of the usual bumps in the road. She calls herself the Chief Bag Lady. In truth, Repke could call herself the chief problem solver. After years of working in the corporate world, primarily in new product development and new product launches, she took the flying leap into her own start-up (*www.coakleybusinessclass.com*).

Who were her greatest influences? Her parents—especially her mother, a professional working woman who balanced family and career. Her father always supported her mother. "They gave me the feeling I could do what I wanted to do," Repke confides. Her bosses? Yes, she was fortunate to have mentors who could help her get the next job. Their faith in her enabled her to push and to gain confidence and trust. Her jobs gave her the foundation for successful entrepreneurship. She had a successful corporate career first.

What about her advisors, her team? Repke acknowledges that for the first couple of years she did it on her own. She went through a session with a business coach and determined that she had to create her ideal job since it did not exist. "My favorite part of my jobs were product development and marketing. I was always running someone else's vision. I enjoyed creating fun, useful products. I had to figure out what that was."

Then, in 2002, while on numerous business trips, annoyed by the minimization of luggage when flying in the post-9/11 environment when the airlines downsized planes, Repke became frustrated by not having the right bag. Then came the two-bag limit. She interviewed women, surveying them right on the plane. She found a high level of interest for a solution to the baggage problem. She did extensive due diligence and focus groups. Repke was passionate about fixing the problem.

Several of her former CEOs and CFOs rallied to give advice; some even offered to invest money. She built a network of people she had worked with who could be part of a company in the absence of the financials. Most of them stepped up to the plate. People worked on a pro-bono basis at the beginning. An accountant and a law firm gave great feedback. She got a good patent law firm. She used professional networking organizations.

But simply having a great idea for a product does not build a great company. How do you fill in the missing pieces? What pitfalls do you avoid? Repke had a full background in manufacturing, marketing, and supply, but not in finance. She sought out a financial advisory board for herself. Many people fail to set up a daily and weekly cash-flow plan. You need to ask yourself how much money you need to do things against what you are bringing in. Properly funding your company from the get-go is critical to your success.

Repke admits, "I had presuppositions that people didn't have money to offer—then they came to me. I got an SBA loan. It was smaller than I wanted; this made it impossible to go for additional funding through traditional moeans. Now, banks want to do business with me." She cautions, "Factoring is only good if you are already established enough and able to return the cash quickly enough. I did venture capital elevator pitches; I wanted to learn the process. It's good to get preapproved in writing. That validates your business to other lenders. When I did a four-year plan, it changed how I wanted to finance the company. Most people don't. My goal is now my exit strategy."

Repke took a course with the Women's Business Center offered by the New Jersey Association of Women Business Owners (NJAWBO). The course showed a grid of an entrepreneur versus a self-employed person. You need to ask yourself, "Is it going to give you your retirement plan? What are you in it for? The fun and the sizzle is creating a product; success is not overnight."

Repke refers to the hidden part. She spent a full year doing due diligence and product development first. She learned that she had a bigger opportunity than she originally even envisioned—fashion, color, and flexibility of sizes are making her successful now. It's a lifestyle bag, not just a laptop bag. She wanted it to be a bag for use all week long. Repke came out of technology, which helped her understand what people carry and their baggage needs. Women are buying two to four bags each, attracted to the idea of seasonal fashion-color choices. The bags are both utilitarian and pretty.

So, what's next for the Chief Bag Lady? Probably a men's bag, with a backpack to follow. Repke asserts that taking in the feedback is important. Patents will add value to the business, as well.

What was the single best business decision she ever made? Pulling in two people on a contract basis to help her get sales and marketing to bring in a sueded textile fabric. It was previously used for outdoor furniture—which made it washable, durable, antimicrobial—and available in many colors. These became the hottest bags, even at a higher price. They opened the door to department stores as well as celebrity merchandising. This is going to be the killer application. Not bad, at about $425.

Repke's advice on a growth strategy? Have the big plan and get methodical about how you are going to implement it. She started with just one channel of trade to begin with (high-end luggage stores, carrying the product they needed to switch from). Then get national, to get national press. Reach a market in a couple of different ways. The press coverage validated her company. Now, she is getting into high-end department stores.

Entrepreneurs need to be focused to succeed. See what sticks and what succeeds. Have a business plan; it makes you think about these issues, and it can change when it needs to. Revisit your plan quarterly and make sure you are on track and that it is working for you. Have a lot of patience. It's too easy to get caught up in the details. You will get buried and can get derailed. Say no to some opportunities; stay focused on the big picture.

As a start-up, each of us needs to choose his unique path. In Repke's case, she went lean. She advises: "Know yourself as a person, what it takes to stay motivated. Give yourself the resources you need. Recognize you are going to have a bad day; get yourself out of it. Do something you really love. Think long and hard about partnerships and the legal and financial aspects. Seek advice early from counsel. Put legal structure in place from the beginning. Know when to get help and how to ask for it. Know what you don't know."

Randy Balcom: Find Your Own Style

Randy Balcom, founder of Style for Life (*www.mystyleforlife .com*), feels compelled to share his success with those who follow him. Earlier, we told you about CEO Space. Balcom derives some of his spiritual feelings about sharing success with others from his experience in the CEO Space program. Speaking of space programs, his company sells an exercise solution originally developed for astronauts—Russian cosmonauts, to be exact. It offers people the opportunity to get the exercise they need quickly, in a small space, without any great strain.

He terms CEO Space, "An awesome networking opportunity. It encourages people to open up their own personal network to help others. A coach has hammered home to me to look at how I can help others first. Just ask them what they need." Balcom networks in his community through a local chapter of BNI plus his local Chambers of Commerce.

As for coaching CEOs in other start-ups, he remarks, "I have an innate talent to help others clarify their vision. I listen to what you need, regurgitate back in language more succinct and focused, and let them say it back to me. It's informal; you pay it forward. No one did it for me."

On the difficult task of finding business coaches that can really help you, Balcom advises you to, "Set out project time lines and deliverables for them. If they don't come through, move on." You have to use some instinct, which he contends is a developed skill. A good business CEO has a finely tuned radar. Balcom favors this model: Jay Abraham takes a percentage of increase in sales. Balcom has set up his company with four board members identified—an attorney, a doctor, a personal coach, a strategic advisor—all high-level people who believe in what he is doing. He remarks, "If they execute on the business plan, we will all make a lot of money. Share the wealth; bring people on who are smarter than you are."

What was Balcom's single best business decision, in his estimation? He focused on personal growth first. In his words, "If you're clear mentally and spiritually as a leader it's so much easier to execute on your plan. I meditate every day; I'm laser focused and waste less time."

What mistakes did Balcom make and how did he correct them? "I created too much overhead without the necessary sales. I had to redirect, so I have to create a large buffer. We will always keep 30 percent plus, cash in the bank."

What did he learn in his prior business life and how did it help him with Style for Life? Balcom previously worked for a *Fortune* 500 company. That experience helped him learn how to grow a cohesive whole; how they function and grow. They knew how to bring in the right people, he contends.

Now that his business has some traction, he is strategizing the company to survive indefinitely, in terms of cash flow. "Our product doesn't require research and development. We are at the early adopter stage; we don't have to compete on price yet. We have good margins; we don't have to raise cash. We are experimenting with telecommuting for our staff. We seek to find the people, those who are independently motivated. We also expect to outsource 90 percent." Notice how clear his vision is—it includes no guesswork at all.

As for product, since much of the production is outsourced, in order to protect their intellectual property they split up the manufacturing across two different companies. Balcom acknowledges that the current product Style for Life sells has a short life cycle. He expects major competition and will have to stay ahead of them. The consumer wants a high-touch experience. His competitors in the exercise equipment industry don't know how to deliver that experience. The current home-fitness model does not address the motivation and support consumers need and want.

Style for Life's points of difference don't end with a unique product. Balcom's marketing plan seeks to get the product into the consumer's hands, find out what they want in their lives, and address it. They seek to make it really fun. For the present, his company will focus on the region they know best—their home market, the Pacific Northwest. However, he has already thought through how to tweak his marketing message for others. For example, the New York market is stressed and time compressed. His product appeals to that; Style for Life offers compression of time. The company will focus on the consumer with the most pain and need for what it offers. They are changing the way people think about exercise.

Here is Balcom's advice to start-ups:

- Slow down and do it right. Don't rush into it.
- Respect the challenge. The odds are against you.

- Walk away from your comfort zone.

"I went to everyone smarter than I was and asked them how to do it. Start-ups get focused on what they think will work and ignore what will work."

- Align with the way today's business is being conducted.

Dr. Jeffrey Magee: Own a Niche

At a time when magazines fold each year, Dr. Jeffrey Magee is launching his into the stratosphere (*www.theperformance magazine.com*). So, how did he do it? Magee founded a magazine for success-minded people and invited the most successful people to pen columns. Each is a brief 500 word how-to article. The publication offers advice from the C-level business executive. It already has an impressive 460,000 subscribers. Subscriber driven, the magazine delivers advice from well-known, high-profile people. There are no features, no trends. In addition, *The Performance* magazine offers regional editions with localized content.

Magee filled a niche no other magazines did—one with highly focused content. One of its predecessors, *Success*, became part of a multilevel marketing company, leaving a void. Magee has positioned the publication with "great content and great people," describing it as a magazine, "where successful people speak for themselves." He has extended the franchise with an Internet radio show, podcasts, live seminars, and coaching to complement the magazine.

What advice does Magee offer to start-ups?

- Don't try to be someone else.
- Every opportunity must be consistent with your vision statement.

- Have a diverse advisory board with trustworthy people.
- Don't overplan before you execute.

Magee's advice to the start-up:

- Work from your passion.
- Assess your skills, training, knowledge, and experience. See what they have to draw upon for that passion.
- Find out how much money it will take and have two to three times that before you start.
- Have documents as strong as a prenuptial agreement. Be the first and the last person to sign every document.

Dan Sterling: From Engineer to Entrepreneur

Dan Sterling of SterlingTech Software (*www.SterlingTech Software.com* and *www.SterlingStart.com* for funding) trained as an electrical engineer and worked for aerospace companies before starting his own company. He developed safety-critical software for aircraft. Then in 1995 he worked as a consultant on medical devices. Dan started Sterling Tech in 1998. In 2003, the company had only five people, and then hired an employee who contributed as a partner. Eventually, he became a partner. Now, the staff numbers twenty people. Sterling went from just one project to handling six to eight projects. It functions as a service company, developing software for others—for device manufacturers or for medical device original equipment manufacturers (OEMs).

What accounted for Sterling Tech's rapid growth? According to Sterling, the company brought in the right people at the right time. He had to give people the right compensation to entice them—even if it looked really high. Flexibility motivates people. Sterling has offered its employees flex-time hours and an hourly rate of pay instead of flat pay like most companies in his field. He further cites having technologically challenging projects as stimulating and interesting, which attract and retain tech talent. Sterling also plans to put in a gym. Most importantly, Sterling is not a layered organization: "You have to be willing to part with a piece of your company. You have to grow the pie for everything. Most entrepreneurs that fail try to hold on to everything. Whatever you do, don't dilute your focus."

Dan Sterling's advice: He cites Robert Kiyosaki: "Don't skimp on the people advising you." Find good advisors and use them—accounting people, a mentor who built a company, those experienced in entrepreneurship. Take the advice from the right people. Seek out those who have done it several times. Don't try to do it all yourself.

Sterling confides that he would have started earlier if he could have. "You have to be a risk taker. Shake the safety thought of working for someone else. I learned where the market is by doing. Be willing to try and fail. Give out work to an expert if you need to. There is a big overhead in managing people. Our largest client has only three employees." Finally, "We do what we know how to do best—execute software."

What about the need to think globally in today's world? Sterling expects competition from the former Soviet Union and from India; however, he points out there are time zone issues with overseas management. Sterling Tech does not outsource anything; their customers are afraid of their intellectual property going offshore. In some cases, subcomponents are built by different people. With the dollar down in value, Europeans see them as a bargain.

What about growth? "Start-ups are always looking for the next round of funding. We have helped them get to the next step with prototypes, etc. We have used creative financing by helping them write grants. In New Jersey, companies can partner with start-ups and get grants. It's the American spirit. Sterling helped one company get their FDA approval; now, investors are coming in. They helped a company go through their clinical studies. Using the devices we produced for them, they got enough data to convince an investor to give them twenty million dollars."

As to resources, Sterling advises companies must develop their technology before going to investors—they can go to state and federal programs for grants first. He recommends SBIR grants and STTR grants from Universities. See *www.grants.gov* for federal government grants. He finds Ohio friendly to funding start-ups, mostly technology; New Jersey for life sciences and energy. He also recommends angel investor groups centered around law firms, including Jumpstart in the Princeton, New Jersey, area; Tri-State Private Investor Network in the New York metropolitan area; and the Venture Association of New Jersey (VANJ); as well as *www.NJEntrepreneur.com*.

What does Sterling term his single best business decision? Hiring his number one employee; giving him anything he wanted to bring him in and make him happy.

His single worst decision? He made a cash investment in a start-up without enough due diligence. He invested in someone who had the wrong motives for starting a company. It should be to make money rather than to get recognition for their technical ability. In his own words, "Finding the right advisor would have saved me a lot."

Neen James: Starting and Restarting

Neen James, a professional public speaker (*www.neenjames.com*), recalls her experience as a two-time start-up—originally in her native Australia and again when she emigrated to the United States, settling in the Philadelphia area. James cites her greatest obstacle to doing a start-up: going from the trappings of a corporate career and infrastructure—she mistakenly took it for granted. She had to make a mental shift and start to create that infrastructure, first by employing a virtual assistant. James's admitted biggest mistake at start-up: not doing the cash projections early enough and not understanding how much income she needed to draw money out, and not getting financial advice early enough. James never wanted to borrow; she wanted to generate what she needed to spend. She overcame the obstacle by seeking advice—outsourced bookkeeping help—and educating herself. She points out, "When it comes to your own business, you notice every dollar." She advises you read books and accelerate your learning.

When she restarted her speaking business in the United States, no one knew James. Plus, the speaking industry in the United States is massive. She had to recreate a whole new business. Fortunately, she didn't make the same mistakes. She reflects back on it as an opportunity: "I got to create my new environment. In just two years, I feel more successful. I had no funding from anyone else. I did it through networking. I targeted women's networks." At the first event she attended, within ten minutes she had landed her first speaking engagement. From then on, James immersed herself completely. She authored a book entitled *Network or Perish*. By joining organizations and working within them, her speaking practice grew. She states, "If I am a 100 percent authentic on the platform, and am there to help, and ask who I need to meet, people open their Rolodexes to me."

From there, James helped others grow their businesses. She recommends *www.EWomenNetwork.com*. Get involved, show up, volunteer. Help others grow their businesses; pay it forward, it will come back to you a hundredfold. Relationships take time.

So, what is our Aussie friend's advice?

- **Create a business plan first.** Invest the money and get someone to help you. Besides financial direction and goals, it helps you assess your strengths and your environment. Consider bartering for it if you can't afford it. Make it a plan that you implement and exercise.
- **Don't listen to the people who don't agree with what you're doing.** If you've done your research and believe in your product, surround yourself with the people who do support you.
- **Get a coach.** How do you choose one? They better look successful and walk the talk. I hired someone who had been in business with a track record and a client list as well as corporate experience. I wanted someone to hold me accountable to my goals. Someone you are going to listen to and respect, someone who will challenge you. They should have a coach themselves.
- **Develop a mastermind group early; it acts like a board of directors.** They have my best interests at heart and they provide me with perspectives. We share our successes and our challenges. They should be people of different genders and experiences.
- **Create product early in your business**—a book, white papers, a CD—especially if you sell intangibles.
- **Look like you deserve your fee.** Make quality choices and decisions. Engage in longer-term thinking—the quality of people you surround yourself with can be a virtual team. Make sure even your business card is quality, your website, your clothing. I hired a publicist since no one knew me. Dedicate at least two hours weekly to PR—publish on free websites, articles. Every business owner should have a one-sheet. Have an editor that can script it professionally. Barter in the early days, if you can.
- **Ask more questions of the client before you determine if you want to work with them.** Choose clients more carefully.

Charlie Stroller: Way Out of the Box

Charlie Stroller, CEO of Charter Financial Publishing Network, had a phenomenal rise to success (*www.cfpn.com*). Let's see what contributed to Stroller's blowtorch effect in business. Before going out on his own, he worked for an American Stock Exchange medical company. In short, he learned what not to do. The company was distressed. Stroller bought half of the company. It was his best training. He cut out the excesses—the overstaffing. He ran lean and mean. Contrary to conventional thinking in corporate America, Stroller says, "If you give people a budget, they spend up to it." Instead, he operates on a principle of "Spend what you need, but don't spend any more than what you would if it were your own company." "People laugh at me—a finance guy with no budgets."

Stroller has done an incredible job of attracting and retaining people. Why? "Some have equity; they work as owners, not employees, plus, they get dividend checks. Sharing the wealth works when you give both raises and bonuses." He refers to Lee Iacocca, who spoke of the "equality of suffering" while at Chrysler. Everybody shared equally in the tough times and the good times. Charlie also points to Charter Financial's casual atmosphere—the dress code, the half-day Fridays in summer: "They like it better when the boss is here than not here. I'll bring in lunch; we have a college dormitory atmosphere. It's congenial."

How does Charter Financial Publishing assemble its team? Hiring the right people is important. Most of the people in the company participate in the decisions—they meet the applicants and give feedback. The proof? Charter has almost no turnover—only for maternity leave. Notably, the rest of the industry has high turnover, especially in sales. Charter has had the same people since 1987. Less turnover equals more success with continuity.

So, what is Charter Financial Publishing's point of difference? According to Stroller, "Everyone is coming to us to partner with. It's the positive word of mouth in the industry. It must be win-win.

We have no contracts with our joint ventures—newsletters and conferences. We give everyone a fair shake. I want to make money with you, not on you. If either party is not happy, they should be able to leave. Our sales people are not doing forecasts and budgets, they're just selling. We practice quick decision making."

It may seem iconoclastic and fly in the face of what everyone else does and preaches, but for Charter Financial Publishing, it works. Charter has eclipsed its competitors in the financial publishing world and expanded a single magazine into a well-respected company with prestigious newsletters, four conferences a year, and now book publishing, as well.

So, what is Stroller's take on doing business today and in the future? With the online competition for magazines, Charter Financial has had to monetize its own online properties. They are doing webinars now, and finding them highly profitable. Stroller's advice to start-ups:

- Hire good people. If possible, hire people you worked with in the past.
- Watch every penny. Don't spend what you don't have to. Spend what you have to spend.
- Take care of your employees. Keep them happy.
- Make your partners happy—win-win.
- Entice new clients; be flexible with them. Engender loyalty.
- Don't spend too much time on budgets, meetings, forecasts—just get out there and make money.

Five Reasons Why 600,000 People a Year Choose to Start Businesses: It's Not Always about the Money

According to Scott Shane, the A. Malachi Mixon professor of entrepreneurial studies at Case Western Reserve University and the author of seven books on entrepreneurship, the economic realities of doing a start-up are more than a little daunting. In his research Professor Shane notes that many entrepreneurs make less money than they might make in their corporate jobs. Shane notes that while, "entrepreneurship creates a lot of wealth it is very unevenly distributed." Shane also notes that starting a business isn't easy. As he writes in a published Internet blog, "Most people who begin the process of starting a business, fail to get one up and running."

Yet, more than 600,000 new businesses are started every year, even though the odds are tough and the economic rewards may not be all that we wish. Here are some of the reasons we believe motivate entrepreneurs to take the plunge no matter the risk.

- **Freedom and the desire to be my own boss.** Perhaps the number one reason that people start up businesses is that they want the freedom to pursue their own dreams, and owning a business in which they can determine how hard or how little they work, how much they risk, and how much they are willing to commit of their personal energies and talents seems better than working for other people. In a very real way, for many folks, even making less money in a situation they control is more attractive than working in a nine-to-five job where they have little or no control.

The number one reason for becoming an entrepreneur is that for many people the quality of their lives goes up. This may not be true in a purely economic sense, as Shane points out, but put in its simplest terms, people start their own businesses and keep at them because they are happier as entrepreneurs than as employees.

- **I've got a great concept that may be risky, but if I don't try I'll regret it forever.** Becoming an entrepreneur for many is an absolute act of faith—faith in themselves, their idea and business concept, and that they can beat the odds. Often the passion that drives an entrepreneur is like the passion that drives any true believer. No matter what reason and statistics and evidence say, the entrepreneur believes through hard work and the power of her concept she can succeed where others fail. And there is always the idea that, "If I don't do this, someone else will, and that will just kill me."

Riding motorcycles fast may be statistically dangerous, but for the Harley-Davidson enthusiast the exhilaration that comes from the ride is worth the risk. So, too, for many entrepreneurs.

- **Wealth creation:** Owning a business can make more wealth than working for a company. While the downside in starting a business is always there, so, too is the upside. While it may be statistically rare, the stories of entrepreneurs who hit the home run engage our imaginations in ways that working for a salary never can. We may know the odds of winning in a start-up are difficult, but they are better than any other gamble we can make, and in the start-up we at least get a chance to shape the results, our destiny, and our financial rewards. And even if our businesses never create great wealth, there are tax advantages to owning your own business that can help many achieve a better standard of living than they would achieve working as an employee.
- **It's in our American blood:** conquering new frontiers. In 1893, the historian Frederick Jackson Turner published his groundbreaking Frontier Thesis that offered his interpretation of why Americans were so different from Europeans. Basically, Turner said Americans constantly had the chance to explore new frontiers and that frontier orientation created an attitude of risk taking and "exceptionalism" that was unique in the world. As our geographic frontiers

shrink, starting new businesses is a new way to go where no one has ever gone before.

Sure there are risks, but the idea of taming the new frontier of a business start-up, of bringing our own skills to bear to do what no one else has done, seems almost natural to many of us. Starting new businesses may be the quintessentially American task in the twenty-first century. While we may not be able to be astronauts or pioneers in a geographic sense, being an entrepreneur is in some ways a heroic endeavor. And who doesn't want to be a hero?

- **Regular jobs just aren't that great.** There is a reason why jobs are called work and not play. And for many of us the tradeoffs that made working in a large company more acceptable have become less and less common. Those traditional benefits that large companies offered to workers like lifetime security, pensions, healthcare, promised promotions, and a predictable future all sound like something out of a past America. If we can lose a job in corporate America, if there is no guaranteed pension, if there is no predictable future in large companies, how can it be worse in my own business?

Sure start-ups are risky, but in a changing global economy the cant phrase used by so many politicians—good jobs at good wages—rings increasingly hollow. We all know there is risk in any company, in any industry, from mergers, acquisitions, global outsourcing. In some ways, owning your own business is the only sure way you'll never be downsized again.

Appendix

B

Sample Private Placement Memorandum

The following is a sample of opening pages from a private placement memorandum (PPM), the key document used in raising funding for many start-ups. It is provided as an example only and in incomplete form, to give the reader a feel for what this document would include. It is not intended as a model to be duplicated. Constructing a PPM requires the work of a securities attorney and your management team.

CONFIDENTIAL PRIVATE PLACEMENT MEMORANDUM

$500,000 of Convertible Notes

Omnibase Logic, Inc., a Nevada corporation (the "Company" or "Omnibase Logic"), offers for sale $500,000 principal value subordinated convertible callable working capital notes bearing simple interest at 15% per annum, compounded and payable according to its terms with maturity in 48 months from issue (the "Convertible Notes"). The Holder of the Convertible Note may convert the principal and interest into shares of Common Stock of the Company at the exchange rate of one share for each $1.00 of principal and interest. The Convertible Notes may be called or converted and exchanged for Common Stock of the Company upon 30 days notice from the Company.

Each note holder shall also have the right of first refusal to participate in any investment or equity program in which the Company participates, such as a joint venture, public company offerings of subsidiaries, etc.

Each convertible note is accompanied by a warrant, valid for 60 months, to purchase 1 share of Omnibase Logic, Inc. common stock at $1.15 per share for each dollar of principal plus accrued interest of the note.

There is no established trading market for the Convertible Notes of the Company offered through this Memorandum or the Common Stock received upon conversion, if any, and none is contemplated. The Convertible Notes are evidences of debt of the Company. The terms of the Convertible Note and the conversion rate were established by management of the Company based on its assessment of the condition of the Company and the future prospects of the Company.

Offering (1)	Principal	Proceeds to the Company (2)(3)
Convertible Notes Offered	$500,000	$500,000
(See Notes on following page)		

THE SECURITIES OFFERED HEREIN INVOLVE A HIGH DEGREE OF RISK. SEE "RISK FACTORS."

NEITHER THE UNITED STATES SECURITIES AND EXCHANGE COMMISSION NOR ANY STATE SECURITIES ADMINISTRATOR HAS APPROVED OR DISAPPROVED THE SECURITIES OFFERED HEREIN NOR HAS THE COMMISSION OR ANY STATE SECURITIES ADMINISTRATOR PASSED UPON THE ADEQUACY OR ACCURACY OF THE DISCLOSURES CONTAINED IN THIS CONFIDENTIAL PRIVATE PLACEMENT MEMORANDUM OR THE MERITS OF AN INVESTMENT IN THE SECURITIES OFFERED HEREIN. ANY REPRESENTATION TO THE CONTRARY IS A CRIMINAL OFFENSE.

THE SECURITIES OFFERED HEREBY HAVE NOT BEEN REGISTERED UNDER THE SECURITIES ACT OF 1933, AS AMENDED, OR THE SECURITIES LAWS OF ANY STATE AND ARE BEING OFFERED IN RELIANCE UPON CERTAIN EXEMPTIONS FROM REGISTRATION UNDER SUCH LAWS. SUCH EXEMPTIONS IMPOSE SUBSTANTIAL RESTRICTIONS ON THE SUBSEQUENT TRANSFER OF SECURITIES SUCH THAT AN INVESTOR HEREIN MAY NOT SUBSEQUENTLY

RESELL THE SECURITIES OFFERED HEREIN UNLESS THE COMMON STOCK IS SUBSEQUENTLY REGISTERED UNDER APPLICABLE FEDERAL AND STATE SECURITIES LAWS OR AN EXEMPTION FROM SUCH REGISTRATION IS AVAILABLE. SEE "RISK FACTORS" AND "SUITABILITY STANDARDS."

The date of this Memorandum is October 31, 2007

1. The minimum investment will be $5,000 for $5,000 principal value Convertible Notes, which will be payable in full in cash upon acceptance of the Subscription. The Company, in its discretion, may accept subscriptions for Convertible Notes in any amount less than $5,000.

2. The Convertible Notes are being offered on a "best efforts" basis by various members of management of the Company and/or by selected brokers/dealers. The Company may agree to pay selling commissions in an amount not to exceed a maximum of ten percent (10%) of the purchase price of the Convertible Notes sold.

3. Before deducting certain offering expenses incurred in connection with the offering of Common Stock, including but not limited to legal fees, accounting fees, printing costs, and state and federal filing fees, if any. The Company estimates these fees and expenses will not exceed $10,000.

The offering of Convertible Notes herein will terminate on December 31, 2007 (unless the Offering is extended by the Company), or in the event that the Company has accepted subscription for $500,000 in the aggregate or the Company terminates the Offering at an earlier date. The checks shall be made payable to OMNI-BASE LOGIC INC., and the checks will be deposited in said account. The Company will apply the funds for the purposes described in this Memorandum.

Appendix

C

Reference Guide for Start-Ups

GENERAL INFORMATION ON START-UP ISSUES

+ **Business.Gov:** The official site of the U.S. government dedicated to advice and services for business start-ups. At this site you can find information on small business grants and loans, how to incorporate a business, how to start a home-based business, how to get started as a government contractor, how to register a business name (doing business as, or "dba"), and many other important and specific topics.

  www.business.gov

+ **Inc.com:** "The Daily Resource for Entrepreneurs." A daily version of the information in the popular magazine that includes success stories, tips, and resources.

  www.inc.com

+ **All Business.com:** A powerful website that contains detailed information about both big and small business issues.

  www.allbusiness.com

+ **Small Business Administration:** The official website of the United States Small Business Administration. It features advice, training programs, and of special value, a listing of local resources and special programs for veterans and reservists of the United States military.

  www.sba.gov

FRANCHISING

- **International Franchise Association (IFA):** Holds regional expos for franchisors and franchisees to connect, publishes a magazine, and holds training seminars.

  www.franchise.org

  1501 K Street NW
  Washington, DC 20005
  202-628-8000

- **The Entrepreneur's Source:** Locally franchised; helps match individuals to franchises they are best suited for.

  www.theesource.com

STAFFING AND ADMINISTRATION SERVICES

- **Administaff**

  www.administaff.com

  1-800-465-3800

- **Accountemps:** to hire financial professionals, book-keepers, and accountants. A division of Robert Half International.

  www.accountemps.com

  1-800-803-8367

- **National Association of Professional Employer Organizations:** for referral to other staffing companies.

  www.NAPEO.org

  901 N. Pitt Street, Suite 150
  Alexandria, VA 22314
  703-836-0466

FUNDING

- **Angel Funding for Emerging Companies:** An Overview

The Houston Angel Network is a good example of a major city angel network. The way they present themselves gives a good understanding of what angel groups are about. Here's how they describe themselves on their website:

"The Houston Angel Network is a nonprofit organization that provides its members a forum in which to efficiently evaluate promising early-stage investment opportunities. Its membership consists of active and SEC-accredited angel investors who share the goal of making informed, collaborative investments in promising early stage Texas-based companies. HAN was founded in late 2001 and is the largest and most active angel network in Texas: Since inception, our members have invested more than $27M in 54 deals."

Members join HAN to:

- Gain access to and invest in prescreened early stage companies in a variety of industries

- Enjoy the benefits of investing with other angel investors sharing due diligence work and deal support
- Gain access to networking and social events that enable them to form relationships and share business opportunities with other successful early stage investors

Companies come to HAN for funding because we offer:

- The opportunity to present to a large group of active and accredited angel investors
- Cash and strategic support from experienced investors with relevant operating experience
- Mentoring and coaching, as well as validation of their business plan

Sponsors join HAN to:

- Form relationships with HAN members, which could result in business opportunities
- View early stage companies which might need the sponsor's services
- Participate in HAN educational events and selected social events

To learn about the Houston Angel Network, go to their website at *www.houstonangelnetwork.com*.

Finding Angel Networks in Your State

Gaebler Ventures hosts a website that provides a list of angel funds on a state-by-state basis. This is a very good model because many angel groups prefer to fund businesses in their own geographic areas. While limited—it certainly does not provide every angel group in any state—it has these advantages over other angel locator sites: it is free and there are no strings attached. The Gaebler list is certainly a good first place to start familiarizing yourself with the world of angel funding. Go to *www.gaebler .com/angel-investor-networks.htm*.

There are many groups who can help raise early stage capital. To get a sense of what they may look like you may want to visit the website of one of the firms mentioned in this book. Please understand, these are just a sample of firms you may want to contact.

Appendix

D

Executive Summary Template

This template is one used by Starlight Capital at their private equity forums, and is used with their permission. They feel so strongly about this format that they require all of the firms seeking funding at their forums to use this model. There are many other approaches that could be used, but the focus on brevity and providing essential information in two pages or less are attributes of executive summaries that would be applauded by most in the venture community. To use this template, replace parenthetical information with your own. This executive summary should be two pages long for at-a-glance ease of potential investors. Wordiness is NOT advantageous. Feel free to bold or underline key points like $, %, and #s.

(Your logo here)

INFORMATION AT A GLANCE
Address:
Phone:
Fax:
E-mail:
Website:
Industry(ies): (Many investors specialize. List markets represented—medical, life science, and technology)
Bank:
Auditor/Accountant:
Law Firm(s): (Some firms have several, such as IP, Securities, and Corporate law firms)

INFORMATION AT A GLANCE (CON'T)

Management: (list names and titles only)

Investment to date: (if useful, identify source)

(Your tag line)

(DESCRIPTIONS IN SENTENCES OR BULLET POINTS)

Business Description: (High level summary: Market scope—international or national; market size, market growth rate, problem/opportunity. Business services or products, variety of revenues streams, profit margin, competitive advantage.)

Company Background: (date and state of incorporation, public (cite stock symbol) or private, start-up or profitable, spinoff or stand alone, growth rate.)

Markets: (More detailed description of market size, scope, problems, opportunities)

Management: (Names, titles and pertinent background or expertise, i.e., previous companies started, sold, deep industry experience, contacts, pertinent degrees in engineering, medicine, finance. Feature advisory board only if important, such as invested or committed in some way.)

(Your tag line)

MORE DETAILED INFORMATION

Services/Products/Benefits: (If appropriate, clarify customer base: retail, wholesale, *Fortune* 50 or small businesses, etc.)

Technologies/Special Know-How: (Patented technology, patent pending, proprietary technology or processes)

Distribution Channels: (Internal or outsourced sales team, industry, or independent comarketers, Internet, etc.)

Competition and Competitive Advantages: (faster, better, cheaper services or products compared to identified competitors. A compare/contrast table is often inserted here.)

ACTUAL AND PRO FORMA FINANCIALS

(High-level summary that showcases the financial advantage of your business model: EBIT or EBITDA, Cost/Profit/Margin)

Year 1	Year 2	Year 3

Index